Serfs & Kings

Demystifying Political Economy

Steven Conrad
Serfs and Kings / Demystifying Political Economy

ISBN-13 978-1461167792
ISBN-10 1461167795

Acknowledgement

Serfs and Kings and *Demystifying Political Economy* contain a compilation of many ideas that I consider original. They also derive from an eclectic set of both contemporary and ancient sources. These sources include essays, novels, textbooks, internet articles, movies, speeches and DVD's. They incorporate concepts of ancient Greek philosophy, Biblical passages, and Age of Enlightenment ideology. They also include present day works of research institutes, experts in the fields of religion, philosophy, political science, and conspiracy theory.

While I have attempted to cite references, it would be impossible for me to acknowledge everyone who has contributed in some way, or to attribute every idea from the multitude contained herein with its originator. Therefore, the best I can do is to acknowledge some of the more recent authors and producers who have given me food for thought. To Aaron Russo, G. Edward Griffin, Steven Sora, David Rivera, Dan Brown, Andrew Hitchcock, Congressman Ron Paul, Adam Kokesh, Jim Marrs, Peter Joseph, Murray Rothbard, Pope Benedict XVI, George Orwell, Alex Jones, and The Wachowski Brothers, thanks for your contributions.

Contents

Part Two : Demystifying Political Economy

Part One : Serfs &Kings

Introduction

"Serfs and Kings" is a second attempt on my part to write a thought provoking work on modern day conspiracy theory. Several years in the making, I struggled with whether or not I should attempt undertaking such a project, as I could easily come up with many reasons not to do so. Given the time demands of the everyday struggle, the controversial nature of this subject matter, the unlikelihood of actually getting published, and concerns about being sued for not making proper citations to copyrighted ideas, etc., I often considered just letting it go. However, when I would have conversations with friends or acquaintances about the subject matter, they were always encouraging me to push forward and put the ideas in writing. Ultimately, whatever the outcome of this endeavor, at least I will have some sense of accomplishment, whether published, unpublished, shared with only close acquaintances or who knows...perhaps some strange cult following?

My first literary attempt was a book entitled "The Final Epiphany," written as a novel that incorporated many of the same concepts contained herein into a fictional plot that I hoped would be both enlightening and entertaining. However, my primary purpose in writing fiction, was that I believed it actually had a greater chance of getting published. My sense is that books written on the controversial subject matter contained in this work either often go unpublished, or find their way through some small publishing firm where they are invisible to all except those who know where to look.

While I was able to create a story that I believe would have been both interesting and entertaining, with many twists and unexpected revelations, I realized that I lacked the necessary creative skills to bring the novel to life. While I was disappointed, I should not have been overly surprised, given I have neither formal training, nor experience as a novel writer. I gained a new found respect for those who can pull it off so adeptly. Rather than just drop the idea entirely, I decided to try the straight forward approach...to make an account of those theories and ideas that have intrigued me for many years. As I write this, the biggest question in my mind is whether anyone will publish? For that matter, I also have had doubts as to whether this *should* be published. Questioning basic tenants of our system of government, education and faith can be both disturbing, and easily misconstrued as "unpatriotic" or even "irreligious". Hopefully, neither of these will be attributed to this effort to uncover truth...for truth should withstand all questioning.

Contrary to what some might think as they read this book, I consider myself as typical and solid an American citizen as anyone...maybe not fitting a stereotype or profile of other conspiracy theorists. I have a career in sales and marketing for a Fortune 100 company, consider myself hard working, patriotic, and compassionate toward others. I am a practicing Catholic, the father of two and have been active in coaching sports, and am involved in the schools and community. I spent most of my adult life as a conservative Republican; perhaps would be considered a "neo-con" by many. While I still consider myself a political conservative, as one who still believes in the Constitution and individual liberties, probably most would consider me something else, though I am not sure what.

While I have always had some question in the back of my mind as to the nature of political and economic power base in this country, it is only within the last couple years that I began to realize that there may be so much more behind our politics than meets the eye. As I became more and more aware of statements and positions that were not true or did not make sense, I began a quest of educating myself to alternative explanations. I was absolutely astounded by what I found, all of which was hidden from public view. I will attempt to share these findings with my readers in a way that will hopefully open the doors to greater enlightenment.

I am not an exegete on philosophy, theology, history, political science or economics; all prominent topics in this work. Nor do I have any formal training in writing, which hopefully is not too evident in this self-edited work. My formal education is in chemistry and business. But I am a believer that real freedom only comes through knowing the truth. In this work I put to the test some of the most basic premises, such as, what is truth? What is knowledge? Is something true because it comes from a trusted authority? If so, who is it that we trust? Who controls the truth?

An ancient philosophy espoused thousands of years ago by Socrates still holds true today...that true wisdom is proved through the realization of what we do not know. Using that as a measure, I consider myself quite wise. Socrates also believed that "the unexamined life is not worth living." However, there is a caveat in such examination: you may come to find the world a much different place than you previously believed...If you like the world as it is or find questioning basic tenets of our everyday existence troubling, read no further.

However, it is my hope that you will enjoy reading the various theories, perceptions, and opinions, that I chose to include in this work. Rather than selecting only those that fit into my own bias, I have tried to incorporate a variety of ideas, from the very mundane to very existential, which hopefully makes for more interesting reading. I have no hidden political agenda; only the hope readers become more engaged in the process and learn to question what they see and hear, especially from those in authority. As I have gained from this journey, I hope you will too, as we explore how the systematic control and manipulation of knowledge is what separates us as Serfs and Kings.

Chapter 1 –In the Beginning

It is difficult to facilitate the appropriate mindset for reading this book as it challenges some fundamental views on what we consider knowledge. Perhaps the best place to start is from the beginning…the very beginning.

Since none of us were here at the beginning of the universe, no one knows for sure its origins, nor can we really comprehend this event. To some extent, a persons' view on many current events depends largely on this single event. Those inclined to the Big Bang theory are likely to view things different than Creationists. Both are pretty difficult to reconcile, as we cannot understand the true nature of God, nor is it easy to believe that all of mankind and his creations are the result of some accidental chemistry that took place in some primordial stew. Some have adopted hybrid versions of both theories, ideas which will be discussed in later chapters. I am not looking to offer an assessment of all perspectives, but rather establish a reference point from which to start exploring the nature of what we believe. For example, creationists tend to believe that there is a plan or purpose for our being, while scientific views explain our nature through evolutionary processes. Throughout this book, a recurrent theme will be how fundamental beliefs influence our worldly opinions.

Despite these fundamentally different perspectives, most of us feel pretty confident about what is real in the world around us. We keep ourselves informed, primarily through the major media, as well as direct communication with others. It is probably rare that one would ask oneself, "is what I perceive real?" Or, "can reality be manipulated, and if so, by whom and for what purpose?"

While we probably give little thought to this today, the search for reality dates back to the ancients. In Plato's "Allegory of the Cave", theorized around 400 BC, he makes the point about how perceptions are shaped by sensory response to our surroundings. In this story, we are asked to imagine a group of prisoners who have not had contact with the outside world, living shackled in a cave. There is a wall behind them, and a fire near the cave opening. The prisoners are only able to see what is front of them, which are shadows cast by objects carried over the heads of people moving behind the wall. The allegory goes on to explain that the shadows become the true objects to the prisoners.

Suppose that one prisoner were to be released from the cave. The first thing he would encounter is the blinding light of day. Then, he would begin to see the world as it really is, and that the shadows were merely images cast by objects carried overhead by others. If the prisoner is to return to the cave and explain this reality to the others, he is likely to be greeted by disbelief, thinking perhaps he went crazy. Plato also suggests that the other prisoners would likely want to do harm to the one who brought him into the light.

Perhaps this ancient allegory seems irrelevant today however, the premise has not changed. While the philosophical process of seeking the truth is certainly not as popular as it was in the day of Plato and Socrates, or for that matter, during the Age of Enlightenment that took place in the eighteenth century, there are those who use this allegorical principle to their advantage. Within certain elitist circles, the philosophical principles espoused by Plato, or more recently by Nietzsche, Hegel, and Marx, are still very relevant.

For example, Plato's *Republic* espouses strongly anti-democratic ideals. He believed that people are best ruled by those who have been raised and educated to lead rather than by someone elected by the populace. This simple, but powerful thesis pervades the thinking of the true *behind the scenes* powers.

Much is written about the ancient Greeks and philosophical thought. Greek sophists spent a great deal of effort examining life in order to better understand truth, the metaphysical, and what constitutes the virtuous life. Their surviving works contain many philosophical tools, such as use of dialectic in testing the truth. The Greeks believed that the good of the individual and the State depended upon the examination of the truth, which was derived from knowledge, and knowledge led to virtuous life. While the arts and sports flourished during the time of famous sophists (Socrates, Aristotle, and Plato), they warned the public not be so distracted by such events as to interfere with the examination of truth.

Consider where most of us are today. If we were to have a name for this period in our history, it could possibly be termed the "Age of Distraction." We are consumed by so many outside stimuli, that it is safe to say that hardly anyone takes a critical, questioning look at what is happening around us. Provided our input comes from a trusted source, we blindly accept things at face value.

To return for a moment to the Allegory of the Cave, what images do we see, and under what context? Is it possible that the messages we receive are largely manipulated with the purpose of controlling us? We have an easy time believing that the media spreads propaganda in countries where people are not as free as we, but could the same manipulations be true here? There is very strong evidence to suggest this may be so.

The point to all of this is that in my search for truth, I have discovered very different historical perspectives completely unknown to me. The question then becomes very obvious…what is the truth, and who is telling it?

The implications of this question are of course obvious…if we all shared the same truth, there would be much less conflict in the world. Winston Churchill was correct in pointing out that "the first casualty of any war is the truth". This also implies that we would share the same faiths and likely the same goals for ourselves and others.

Chapter 2 – Some History

If you look history up in the dictionary, you will see at least a half dozen definitions, but most concisely, it can be defined as the story or recording of past events. Along the same lines, we define news as the story of current events. Complete objectivity in the communication of fact surrounding events, current or historical, is very difficult even where well intended. First of all, trying to record facts absent of emotion or perspective can be extremely difficult, and it is said that history is generally written by the victor. In conversation with associates from other countries, it is obvious that they share different perspectives on the same historical event. Throw in inherent language constraints, especially translations into multiple languages, and this further complicates historical perspectives.

Another important factor influencing accuracy is whether those controlling the recording of news and history have an agenda, which greatly increases the likelihood of getting a record of opinion, rather than fact. It is apparent from watching different newscasts that the same event can be spun to seem considerably different based on one's disposition. Most people that I know use the "trusted authority" basis for what they accept as news or historical fact. But, as we shall see, this requires closer examination. We need to take into question what we may have previously accepted as historical fact in the same way we should question alternate, and perhaps "less authoritative" sources, such as those commonly found on the internet.

One should not necessarily pass judgment too hastily as to which sources are more accurate. My findings through various non-conventional sources reveal a history that in some cases looks considerably different than the bland text book version taught in school. What is perhaps more interesting, is that this arcane version often seems more credible, in that it makes more sense. While school taught versions focus on dates and events, they largely miss the underlying motivations behind many historic events, particularly when it comes to wars. They also never address the possible underlying conspiracies that play a very key role in our national and world history.

If we just look at our own nation's history, we find highly varied perspectives if we consider all sources. For example, we typically think of our Founding Fathers as principled idealists who were fundamentally concerned with basic liberties. This view is not universal however, as there are some who would suggest that many were self serving capitalists, concerned more with economic gain than principles. Piracy, smuggling and drug trade were all prevalent in the early years of this country and some of the elite of the time were linked to these trades. In addition, many of the same elite have been connected to secret societies, primarily freemasonry.

In truth, the average person does not have any way of knowing with certainty what is true and what is not. If nothing else, it is interesting to consider some of the alternate views that are out there. It is also difficult to decide where, and at what point in time to begin one's historical perspective. Most texts generally start with the ancient Egyptian civilizations after 3000 BC, or perhaps the civilizations of Sumer, dating back to about 4000 BC. While these are considered the earliest advanced civilizations, some believe advanced civilizations inhabited this planet hundreds of thousands of years prior. Cataclysmic events, such as the comet strike thought to have caused extinction of the dinosaurs may have wiped out earlier advanced civilizations. As an example, such a cataclysmic event may have occurred around 7000 B.C., with a large comet strike in the area of Hudson Bay in Canada, wiping out advanced civilizations that existed at that time. Others have even suggested that it is secret knowledge from these very early civilizations that continues to empower those who now control it.

While archaeologists and historians have assembled an approximation on what ancient civilizations were like and have documented historical facts about some of the more important civilizations and their leaders, one has to wonder how power and control over the early civilizations evolved. While most early records indicate some ancestral authority, it is not clear how the early emperors, kings, queens and pharaohs were initially elevated or anointed to positions of such prominence. How did they become godlike, or how did they derive their authority from an unseen higher authority? While creating an exegesis on the evolution of ruling class authority would certainly be interesting, it is not one that I am equipped to deal with here. In reality, we don't really know what is historical fact, myth, or fiction; only what we are taught in school. Given the limited exposure to history for most, the general impression is that the two fundamental influencing factors in the evolution of power and control throughout the years have been war and religion.

But, aside from what we see as outward changes resulting from war, changes in geographic boundaries, forms of government, religion, etc., we may have missed the subtle changes, which take place out of view, which are not recorded in the textbooks. These are the changes that influence the minds of those governed. It is here where some of the secret societies come into play.

Secret Societies may have played a role in the governing of people for ages. While many political, religious and social organizations originated openly, many were later forced into secrecy, depending upon changes in the political environment at the time. Some societies were formed within governing bodies, while others were considered anti-establishment. There were a number of groups that challenged religious authority. For example, the early Gnostics proposed different ideas about the nature of our dualistic being, i.e., our material vs. spiritual being in early Christian and pre-Christian eras. Another example, occurring in a later era was the Cathars, a growing religious sect in parts of France, who opposed church dogma similar to the earlier Gnostics. Because of the challenge to church authority and resulting persecution, groups from these sects began operating in secrecy.

Medieval Christianity brought about a group that was originally aligned with Church authority known as the Knights Templar, formed around 1100 AD. This group grew in prominence as both a military force, a charitable organization, and also what was probably the first financial organization. The early roots of banking have been connected with the Templars, as they were entrusted with protecting wealth of business people and issuing letters of credit which could be used in areas outside the geography where the actual wealth was held. The issuance of a Templar note represented the actual deposit of valuables.

Templar prominence and management of wealth was thought to be a reason for its eventual demise. Some believe the organization challenged to the authority of the Pope and following the failed Crusades, the church authority took the opportunity to eliminate the Templars. Under Pope Clement V, many Templars were arrested with some burned at the stake. It is believed that factions of the Templars escaped underground to begin new secret societies. Popularized by modern books and movies, some suggest that the Templars were the holders of great treasure, both physical as well as esoteric knowledge obtained during the Crusades. This connection to both knowledge and banking forms the cornerstones of future secret organizations.

The Priory of Sion (or *Prieuré de Sion)* was another related secret organization linked to the Templars. The legend of this cabal became popular in the late 1960's and it was again popularized in modern novels such as in Dan Brown's *Da Vinci Code.* According to legend, this organization protects secrets uncovered by the Crusades that prove a lineage to Jesus Christ still exists through the Merovingian Dynasty and will one day resume authority over a universal church.

There is a great deal of information about these secret organizations in numerous published works, but it is very difficult to sort fact from fiction. Undoubtedly, there existed throughout periods of history, including modern day, secret cabals containing philosophers with the intent of imposing their world view on others. It is also questionable whether their intent is well meaning or self-serving.

Hundreds of years after the Templars came the "Age of Enlightenment," which is the name given to the period of Western philosophical thought in the 18th century or late Renaissance. This period brought about a flood of ideas with widespread implications on religion, governance, freedom, and individual rights. Philosophers such as Immanuel Kant, Gottfried Leibniz, Johann Wolfgang von Goethe, John Locke, Adam Smith, as well as Americans Ben Franklin and Thomas Jefferson all emerged from this period. The primary ideal from this Age is the preeminence of man; where man, not God is the measure of all things. This key precept becomes the foundation not only for scientific development, but also governance and prevails as the underpinning for what is to follow.

Perhaps the most interesting of the secret cabals to spring forth from this era of "enlightenment" was the Illuminati. Founded in Bavaria by Adam Weishaupt in 1776, this group of elitist thinkers had the secret goal of infiltrating and over-throwing governments. There remains much controversy over the history of Weishaupt and the order that he helped create. For many conspiracy theorists, including myself, the Illuminati represent the essence of the modern day elitist "philosopher kings." The goal of Weishaupt and his colleagues was not to control the masses through military means, but rather control their minds and their money. In such a way, he foresaw the possibility to create a New World Order based on his own philosophical beliefs.

Adam Weishaupt was educated in the Jesuit tradition following the death of his father, a rabbi professor at the University of Inglostadt. He was influenced at a young age by Jesuit teaching, but later began exploring other schools of philosophical "enlightenment". There is some contention over whether Weishaupt became anti-Christian, or only opposed religious authority. Some suggest that in his pursuit of enlightenment, Weishaupt had been influenced by the occult, and possibly Satanism. His goals to overthrow governments and organized religion were inspired by his belief that if men could be inspired by morality, virtue and knowledge, they could live free of oppression from authority. However, others believe that there was a more nefarious side to Weishaupt and his view for a New World Order.

Weishaupt has also been portrayed as follower of Lucifer and some have even suggested personal contact with Lucifer. For anyone not familiar with the legend, Lucifer is the name given to the devil as translated from particular scriptural passages. The fallen "morning star," Lucifer was an angel who sought equality with God and was cast out of heaven down to earth, where he became known as Satan. There are those who believe Lucifer or Satan shares secret knowledge with some of his followers, who see him as the "light". It is the use of this esoteric knowledge that enables his followers to control other human beings. As will be discussed later, there are very powerful present day global figures who are believed to also be followers of this same "light". Thus, there is this dualism in "Illuminism," an aspiration toward virtue and freedom that could attract righteous people of influence to be duped into serving to create a New World Order based on Satanic principles. Many people of influence joined the Illuminati as well as others whose motivation to support the Illuminati were based purely on personal greed.

As the Illuminati grew in prominence and its influence spread, the organization, along with all other secret societies, was banned by the Bavarian ruler of the time. The Illuminati found refuge in another organization, Freemasonry, who shared at least some philosophical views as well as the key principal of operating in secrecy. But what gave Weishaupt and his secret organization true power, was his later association with the Rothschilds.

The Rothschild family banking dynasty is one of the most powerful and influential in history. Mayer Amschel Rothschild was the founder of this empire, which was built from very meager beginnings in Germany back in the mid 1700's. Through a series of very strategic investments and alliances with various ruling parties, the empire gained tremendous wealth and power. However, like Weishaupt, there was also a very dark side to this tremendous success story. Like Weishaupt, the builders of the Rothschild empire were also linked to secret cabals and possibly Satanism. The Rothschild fortune was also built on some very unscrupulous deals, i.e., manipulating markets and financing both sides of conflicts.   With the aid of the Illuminati, Rothschild was believed to be the force behind the French Revolution and even the American Revolution. Turning wars into successful business ventures through financing of armies and using the financial leverage to gain additional wealth and power became a very successful formula. By 1800, the empire had spread across Europe with the next step being the creation of a central banking authority in England. This became a fundamental stronghold for the group.

The success of Illuminati / Freemasonry group was not limited to Europe. In the U.S., George Washington, John Adams, and Ben Franklin were prominent early members, as were many of the signers of the Declaration of Independence. As time went on, the power of the secret organization became increasingly troubling for many governments, including the U.S. Laws banning the organization were enacted in effort to prevent it from gaining substantial power over the federal government. Even the Vatican had issued many statements condemning the secret organization for its attempt to undermine governments and organized religion. Unfortunately, through evolution and deeper secrecy, the elitists continued to increase their stranglehold.

Chapter 3 - The Protocols

One of the most disturbing documents attributed to the Illuminati was a document known as The Protocols of the Learned Elders of Zion. The document was believed to be a blueprint of the Illuminati plan for developing a New World Order. The origins of this document are not clear. One story alleges that this document was found on a courier who was struck by lightning some time around the 1860's. Whatever its true origin, this blueprint for world domination became a grave concern to government leaders as it circulated through much of Europe and Russia. The following is an excerpt translated by Victor Marsden:

"Out of the temporary evil we are now compelled to commit, will emerge the good of an unshakable rule, which will restore the regular course of the machinery of the national life, brought to naught by liberalism. The result justifies the means. Let us, however, in our plans, direct our attention not to what is good and moral, as to what is necessary and useful. Our power in the present tottering condition of all forms of power will be more invisible than any other, because it will remain invisible until the moment when it has gained such strength that no cunning can any longer undermine it. Before us is a plan in which is laid down strategically the line from which we cannot deviate without running the risk of seeing the labor of many centuries brought to naught..."

"Only force conquers in political affairs, especially if it be concealed in the talents essential to statesmen...This evil is the one and only means to attain the end, the good. Therefore we must not stop at bribery, deceit, and treachery, when they should serve towards the attainment of our end. In politics one must know how to seize the property of others without hesitation if by it we secure submission and sovereignty."

"Our international rights will then wipe out national rights, in the proper sense of right, and will rule the nations precisely as the civil law of States rules the relations of their subjects among themselves. The administrators, whom we shall choose from among the public, with strict regard to their capacities for servile obedience, will not be persons trained in the art of government, and will therefore easily become pawns in our game in the hands of men of learning and genius who will be their advisors, specialists bred and reared from early childhood to rule the affairs of the whole world."

"Do not suppose for a moment that those statements are empty words: think carefully of the successes we arranged for Darwinism, Marxism, Nietzcheism. To us, at any rate, it should be plain to see what a disintegrating importance these directives have had upon the minds of the goyim(a slur against those who were not Jewish)."

"Through the Press we have gained the power to influence while remaining ourselves in the shade; thanks to the Press we have got the gold in our hands, notwithstanding that we have had to gather it out of the oceans of blood and tears."

"To this end we have stirred up every form of enterprise, we have armed all parties, we have set up authority as a target for every ambition...disorders and bankruptcy will be universal."

"We appear on the scene as alleged saviors of the worker from this oppression when we propose to him to enter the ranks of our fighting forces - Socialists, Anarchists, Communists - to whom we will always give support."

"Our power is in the chronic shortness of food...Hunger creates the right of capital to rule the worker more surely than it was given to the aristocracy by the legal authority of kings."

"By want and the envy and hatred which it engenders we shall move the mobs and with their hands we shall wipe out all those who hinder us...When the hour strikes for our Sovereign Lord of all the World to be crowned it is these same hands which will sweep away everything that might be a hindrance thereto."

"This hatred will be still further magnified by the effects of an economic crisis, which will stop dealings on the exchanges and bring industry to a standstill. We shall create by all the secret subterranean methods open to us and with the aid of gold, which is all in our hands, a universal economic crisis whereby we shall throw upon the streets whole mobs of workers simultaneously in all the countries of Europe."

"Remember the French Revolution, to which it was we who gave the name of 'Great': the secrets of its preparations are well known to us, for it was wholly the work of our hands..."

"We shall create an intensified centralization of government in order to grip in our hands all the forces of the community. We shall regulate mechanically all the actions of the political life of our subjects by new laws...These laws will withdraw one by one all the indulgences and liberties which have been permitted...to wipe out any unenlightened who oppose us by deed or word."

"We have set one against another the personal and national reckonings of the goyim religious and race hatred, which we have fostered into a huge growth in the course of the past twenty centuries. This is the reason why there is one State which would anywhere receive support if it were to raise its arm, for every one of them must bear in mind that any agreement against us would be unprofitable to itself. We are too strong - there is no evading our power. The nations cannot come to even an inconsiderable private agreement without our secretly having a hand in it..."

"Nowadays it is more important to disarm the peoples then to lead them into war..."

"In order to put public opinion into our hands we must bring it into a state of bewilderment by giving expression from all sides to so many contradictory opinions and for such length of time as will suffice to make the goyim lose their heads in the labyrinth and come to see that the best thing is to have no opinion of any kind in matters political, which it is not given to the public to understand, because they are understood only by him who guides the public. This is the final secret."

"By all these means we shall so wear down the goyim that they will be compelled to offer us international power of a nature that by its position will enable us, without any violence, gradually to absorb all the State forces of the world and to form a Super-Government...Its hands will reach out in all directions like nippers and its organization will be of such colossal dimensions that it cannot fail to subdue all the nations of the world."

"We shall raise the rate of wages, which, however, will not bring any advantage to the workers, for at the same time, we shall produce a rise in prices...We shall further undermine artfully and deeply sources of production, by accustoming the workers to anarchy and to drunkedness...In order that the true meaning of things may not strike the unenlightened before the proper time we shall mask it under an alleged ardent desire to serve the working classes and the great principles of political economy about which our economic theories are carrying on an energetic propaganda."

"The intensification of armaments, the increase of police forces - are all essential for the completion of the aforementioned plans. What we have to get at is that there should be in all the States of the world, besides ourselves, only the masses of the proletariat, a few millionaires devoted to our interests, police and soldiers."

"In a word, to sum up our system of keeping the governments of the goyim in Europe in check, we shall show our strength to one of them by terrorist attempts and to all, if we allow the possibility of general rising against us, we shall respond with the guns of America or China or Japan."

"Our directorate must surround itself with all these forces of civilization among which it will have to work. It will surround itself with publicists, practical jurists, administrators, diplomats and, finally, with persons prepared by a special super-educational training in our special schools."

"We have in our service persons of all opinions, of all doctrines, restorating monarchists, demagogues, socialists, communists, and utopian dreamers of every kind. We have harnessed them all to one task: each one of them on his own account is boring away at the last remnants of authority, is striving to overthrow all established forms of order."

"We have fooled, bemused and corrupted the youth of the goyim by rearing them in principles and theories which are known to us to be false although it is by us that they have been inculcated."

"Above the existing laws without altering them, and by merely twisting them into contradictions of interpretations, we have erected something grandiose in the way of results. These results found expression first in the fact that the interpretations masked the laws: afterwards they entirely hid them from the eyes of the government owing to the impossibility of making anything out of the tangled web of legislation."

"The chamber of deputies will provide cover for, will protect, will elect presidents, but we shall take from it the right to propose new, or make changes in existing laws, for this right will be given by us to the responsible president, a puppet in our hands...We shall invest the president with the right of declaring a state of war..."

"Not a single announcement will reach the public without our control. Even now this is already attained by us inasmuch as all news items are received by a few agencies, in whose offices they are focused from all parts of the world. These agencies will then be already entirely ours and will give publicity only to what we dictate to them."

"Our wise men, trained to become leaders of the goyim, will compose speeches, projects, memoirs, articles, which will be used by us to influence the minds of the goyim, directing them towards such understanding and forms of knowledge as have been determined by us."

"Economic crises have been produced by us for the goyim by no other means than the withdrawal of money from circulation...You are aware that the gold standard has been the ruin of the States which adopted it, for it has not been able to satisfy the demands for money, the more so that we have removed gold from circulation as far as possible."

"Thanks to such methods (paying interest on loans), allowed by the carelessness of the goy States, their treasuries are empty. The period of loan supervenes, and that has swallowed up remainders and brought all the goy states to bankruptcy."

"...any form of taxation per head, the State is baling out the last coppers of the poor taxpayers in order to settle accounts with wealthy foreigners, from whom it borrowed money from the pockets of the poor to those of the rich..."

"We have got our hands into the administration of the law, into the conduct of elections, into the press, into the liberty of the person, but principally into education and training as being the corner-stones of a free existence."

"...it is indispensable for us to undermine all faith, to tear of minds out of the unenlightened the very principle of Godhead and the spirit, and to put in its place arithmetical calculations and material needs."

"When we come into our kingdom it will be undesirable for us that there should exist any other religion but ours of the "One God" with whom our destiny is bound up by our position as the Chosen People and through whom our same destiny is united with the destinies of the world. We must therefore sweep away all other forms of belief."[1]

The controversy over the origins and intent of the document makes it very difficult to determine its authenticity or source. Many at the time believed the source to be a secretive Jewish group, while others believe is was adopted from a work by a French author about Napoleon's goals for world domination later adapted as a tool to foment anti Semitism. Some contend that the original work was directed by the Jesuits as those who plotted to take over the world. Whatever the source, the Protocols were troubling for years to follow as fear of world domination and perhaps the coming of the "Antichrist" appeared in many countries throughout, Europe, Russia and other parts of the world.
In researching the Protocols, I also found it disturbing that, according to most sources, the documents had far reaching consequences in terms of their impact. This includes conspiracies connected the French Revolution, the Bolsheviks, the Nazis, as well as conflicts in the Middle East. Yet, before doing this research, I never heard of them or anything about any secret societies that allegedly played such prominent political roles from the mid eighteenth century on. One would think that this would be an integral part of learning history, unless of course, the exclusion is deliberate.
The principles espoused in the Protocols, control of governments, money, media, education, and religion recur throughout

---

[1] David Rivera : A Final Warning – The History of the New World Order
Silverbearcafe.com

this book. Regardless of the origin, the Protocols reflect the true mind of the beast.

Chapter 4 – Money and Banking

It seems a pretty safe assumption that for any group to attain significant power and control, they must have adequate financial backing. Given this connection between wealth and power, it is probably worth spending some time exploring the evolution of money and banking in society. Despite much research on the topic, the origins and evolution of money are somewhat elusive. There is considerable disagreement even among global economic experts on the topic. Rather than provide an in depth historical analysis, I will try and convey some ideas that I believe are relevant.

In its early origins one can think in monetary terms as the trade or barter of items having like value. In time, this was followed by "representation" of something of value by currency. Historical accounts dating back as far as 3000 B.C. describe the acceptance of currency as "money" in commerce. Early currency was generally coinage but could be other commodities as well. In general, money needed to be something easily transportable, non-perishable, and durable, be limited in availability, and have some intrinsic value. In addition, there needed to be rules governing how it was used, how it could be borrowed, and how much interest that could be collected.

The creation of money, its supply and the rules governing its use, really warrants some very careful thought, as its control is at the heart of behind-the-scenes power. Returning to the historical evolution of money and the monetary system, we see an evolution toward money being tied to precious metals, particularly gold and silver. This is because they became a widely accepted medium of exchange for the free market merchants. In this case, a note could be offered by a banking authority, and be redeemed for a certain quantity of the precious metal backing it. There are still proponents of the gold standard, believing that money should be backed by tangible, assayable, limited resources with intrinsic value. Although, in reality, what is the intrinsic value of gold? In reality, it is just a nice, shiny rock that can be used to make jewelry and few other articles. One has to question why it is worth (at the present time) over US$1000/oz.?

The gold standard demise began in Britain long before it took place in the U.S. The issuance of banknotes, which were partially backed by gold or silver became popular for some time, but were later replaced with fiat currencies. These currencies have no intrinsic value and are not backed by anything other than a promise from the governments issuing them. All major currencies are now fiat currency, not backed by any commodity or promise.

In truth, money is an invention of the mind and only works because we are trained to believe it works. To better understand the illusion, it is important to look at the evolution of banking, the powers behind the money. The earliest banks may have predated the origin of money. They were repositories for other items of value, such as crops. A receipt or bank note would be issued and could be redeemed against the deposit. According to some historical sources, ancient Babylon, followed by ancient Greece, had developed organized banking systems with rules governing loans and interest. As the system grew, major religions took a position on the on the charging of interest on debt. These ranged from proclamations banning its practice, to imposing many restrictions, especially against usury. Islam in particular condemns the charging of interest very clearly in the Koran.

Following a long period where banking practices were either non-existent or of little consequence, commercial banking came back into favor during the Crusades. The extensive resources required to finance the Crusades and the need to transfer large sums of money across vast geographic areas, stimulated resurgence in banking. Along with a growing commodities trade in Europe, the need for bank notes, as a way of circumventing the need to move large sums of money over long distances grew. The Knights Templar and Hospitallers became a dominant banking power through Europe to the Holy Land.

Following the failed Crusades there was a growing rift between the Pope and the Knights Templar, who had amassed great wealth and power. With direction from the Pope, King Phillip of France ordered the disbandment of the Knights and the recovery of their wealth. While many of the Knights were persecuted, some escaped to Scotland where remnants of the order are connected with the latter Freemasons.

According to historical records, prominent members of the church hierarchy became very successful bankers. This was particularly true of the Medici family of Florence. This family was not only very successful in business and banking, but produced four Popes.

In addition to centers in France and Italy, banking centers also grew in Germany and Britain. Many of the money changers, the predecessor of the bankers, were Jews. These were considered lowly positions, akin to a tax collector, and were given to the Jews who were considered societal outcasts at the time. The other important factor in the prominence of Jewish banking was that the Jews were not governed by the harsh usury laws imposed by church hierarchy. However, out of a very humble beginning, arose probably the most influential banking families in all of Europe, the Rothschilds.

The Rothschild banking dynasty was started by Meyer Amschel Rothschild. Born in Germany in 1744, Rothschild and his sons built an incredibly powerful dynasty from the very humble origins in the Jewish ghetto. Beginning in Frankfurt in 1763, Meyer and his five sons established an enormous banking position throughout Europe by the turn of the 19th century. Some sources credit very astute business acumen behind the success, but most have attributed the success to completely unscrupulous business practices. This included secretly financing both sides of armed conflicts and leveraging war debt into more money, smuggling, stock market manipulations, etc. Despite its sinister nature, the magnitude of the success was unprecedented. Rothschild influence over governments looking for money continued to grow and at the same time, the family maintained a secret, behind the scenes profile. The mastery of using debt to create money and the use of fractional banking, which is the practice of providing notes that exceed deposits or reserves, was being perfected by this dynasty. Understanding the practice of fractional banking, becomes a key to understanding business cycles, inflation and deflation, and will be discussed in greater detail. It also helps explain how such extraordinary wealth and gold reserves were accumulated from the humble origins of this empire. To put the Rothschild success into perspective, biographer Frederic Morton said that this family had "conquered the world more thoroughly, more cunningly, and much more lastingly than all the Caesars before or all the Hitlers after them."[2]

It was a great time to be in banking, between growing commerce and as the race to colonize and expand resource bases created war upon war. Having the resources to lend was not only profitable because of interest that could be earned, but also the leveraging of favors that would bring even greater economic opportunity, whether trade rights, mineral rights, or even tax breaks. Many very powerful connections were forged during this time, all taking place behind the scenes. It is interesting to note, that Benjamin

---

[2] Frederic Morton, The Rothchilds: A Family Potrait

Disraeli, who served as British Prime Minister from 1874-1880 wrote of this time, "The world is governed by very different personages from what is imagined by those who are not behind the scenes."[3] But perhaps Meyer Rothschild himself summed it up very well in claiming, "Let me issue and control a nation's money and I care not who writes the laws..."[4]

Controlling a nation's money is the principal function of central banking authorities. The first central bank appeared in England at the end of the 17th century. As wars periled government finances, the concept to form a Bank of England was devised by William Paterson. Imbued with many special privileges, a secretive group of bankers put together a deal to finance government debt through the manufacture of fiat money. The English government accepted the idea, considering it preferable to imposing high taxes on the populace, especially following years of civil war. Despite many bank failures, bank runs, suspension of payments (specie payments) and inflation, the model eventually worked and was adopted by other countries. As subordinate banks came to rely on the central banks as the primary repository for reserves, central bank notes became the monopoly legal tender of the country.

In the United States, our Constitution provides for congressional authority over the borrowing, coinage and regulation of monetary value. It also stipulates that all debts must be payable in gold or silver. This draft followed the disastrous monetary experience in trying to finance the Revolutionary War with fiat currency that became ridiculously inflated.

Like Europe, the U.S. had a number of very powerful, well connected merchants interested in following the English banking example. The first attempt to form a central bank was initiated by Congressman Robert Morris in 1781. Based on the same fractional banking model, e.g., the generation of multiples of money based on reserves, the model failed as the notes it generated were not widely accepted and became highly inflated.

The second attempt, ten years later, was much more successful, as the new Bank of the United States had greater backing by the wealthy elitists, including the Rothschilds. However, like the first, the notes generated became highly inflated and this central bank only survived until 1811. Despite the corruption and problems associated with the central banks, the government decided to reauthorize the 2nd

---

[3] Jim Maars, Rule by Secrecy
[4] G. Edward Griffin, The Creature from Jekyll Island

Bank of the United States a few years later.   Again, the monopolistic bank was controlled by a handful of very wealthy Americans, and European financiers.   Then President Andrew Jackson fought successfully against the bank, despite a contrived financial crisis designed by its backers.   Despite this victory, the nation was facing many economic problems helping to push it toward civil war.   It would be foreign interests operating in secrecy that would help promote the cause of this war and most others to follow.

Around the turn of the twentieth century, the wealthy industrial and banking powers were at work once again.   J.P. Morgan, considered the leading force in the move to consolidate U.S. banking authority, spearheaded another banking crisis with the help of other American and European backers.   With the assistance of some well connected political insiders, such as Aldrich Ames, the group was able to resolve the banking crises they had created by putting together the Federal Reserve.   The deal was made in secrecy at Morgan's island off of the coast of Georgia called Jekyll Island, thus giving life to "The Creature from Jekyll Island."[5]   The new Federal Reserved was promoted by government insiders, including then President Woodrow Wilson (who later lamented over his decision) and was passed through Congress as they were beginning Christmas recess.   The Federal Reserve was placed in control of the U.S. monetary system in December 1913.

---

[5] Ibid.

Chapter 5 – Life Under the Federal Reserve

There is much to discuss about the Federal Reserve, the people who control it, and the influence it has over the U.S. economy. In the first place, much to the surprise of many Americans, the Federal Reserve is a legal monopoly that is not run by the government, but rather by powerful American and foreign banking interests. The name "Federal Reserve" was a deliberate deception by its founders to make it appear as a government entity. It has authority over commercial banks, establishing reserve levels as well as "multiplier" levels, i.e., the multiples of reserves a bank can loan. In addition, the Fed acts as the "lender of last resort", and can thereby support banks that run into problems with insufficient funds.

Rather than provide an in depth analysis of the Federal Reserve system, a little history and outline of its primary functions will be helpful in understanding why control over central banking authority is key for those who seek power. In addition to establishing reserve and lending levels, the Fed has a number of other important functions in facilitating inter-bank lending, check clearing, etc. The powers of the Fed have increased over time and now include buying and selling of assets on the open market. But more interesting, it can purchase assets based on money that it prints up from nothing, and use the deposited asset as a reserve. Thus is the power to control the national money supply. Usually, the Fed buys and sells government Treasury bonds, but it can also buy and sell corporate stocks, bonds, foreign currencies, etc.

Fed purchases of US Treasuries have been increasing since its inception. This causes an in increase in money supply, which in turn, by the laws of supply and demand, creates inflation. Many economists agree that this is in fact the leading cause of inflation. The Fed can also use its purchasing power to buy bonds from commercial banks, which then gives the banks additional reserves, which they can in turn use to generate multiples by way of loans.

Under the guidance of the likes of Morgan, Rockefeller and Warburg, the Fed assumed control over gold deposits from the banks, using these reserves to print money to return to the banks. It was in a sense, legal counterfeiting. The early Reserve notes were backed by gold, but later, became only partially backed by gold, and finally, the gold backing was completely eliminated.

Another interesting aspect of the Fed, was that when the government came to the Fed to purchase government debt, the Fed would do so, but charge interest to the government. This on money they printed up like wall paper, essentially out of nothing. Within just a couple of years after the formation of the Fed, a new tax, the Federal Income Tax, came into existence. This tax, which is still debated by many as being unconstitutional, was largely put into place to pay interest on government debt to the Fed.

In addition to being inflationary, as more money is created by the banks based on fractional reserves, there is also a side affect of what we now view as "normal business cycles". This occurs due to the nature of the expansion and contraction of debt and reserves. A major expansion of credit occurred within several years of Fed formation, as bank reserve levels were cut by about half from where they were previously. The influence of expanding capital in the market led to artificially high supported asset price levels, particularly, stock prices. Some suggest this loose monetary policy was adopted by Morgan insiders to support Allied World War I interests. The war generated huge profits for Morgan, who brokered British and French war bonds and supplied munitions. The inflationary pressures in the U.S. were designed to help British interests, tied to Morgan, as they were fighting rampant inflation due to similar banking practices. However, the eventual fallout was the disastrous crash in 1929.

However, the crash of 1929 had an upside for some, as it facilitated considerable consolidation of wealth by the same American and European elitists who were manipulating the economic crisis. Those with the inside knowledge of the pending crash moved their assets to safe havens, such as gold. The head of the House Banking and Currency Committee at the time, Congressman Louis T. McFadden stated:
"It was not accidental. It was a carefully contrived occurrence...The international bankers sought to bring about a condition of despair here so that they might emerge as rulers of us all."[6]

The sentiments that the Great Depression was caused by the actions of the Fed have been agreed upon by many, including such noted economists as Nobel Prize winner Milton Friedman. The

---

[6] Andrew Carrington Hitchcock, The Synagogue of Satan

opportunities to buy up distressed assets, especially stocks of companies that were considered important for securing its power base, such as media, energy, banking, etc. were abundant.

Another important Fed function is to provide much of the financial data that is used by governments, businesses and financial institutions. Indicators on manufacturing, inflation and other indexes come from the Fed. The news released to the markets can be used to paint whatever picture deemed appropriate. For example, core inflation reports can show very benign inflation, because they remove things such as food and energy. It also compares baskets of goods, so that if someone had been buying steaks and Cadillacs, and through reduced spending power started buying hamburgers and Chevrolets at the same prices, this would show as "non inflationary" by Fed measurements. In truth, real purchasing power has been eroding, if one considers the effect of low real interest rates minus inflation and currency depreciation.

As will be discussed later, economic policy driven by the Fed and other central banks will have consequences in future wars and conflicts. They will also play a major role in the distribution of wealth, politics and business. This should not be surprising, given that the balance sheet of the Fed in April 2009 showed assets of about $2.2 trillion.

While the endless debt created under the Federal Reserve System keeps the Federal government and the entire population in eternal debt, politicians would be loath to change anything. For it is with debt they can create programs to keep them popular with the constituents who keep them in office.

Perhaps the symbol on the back of the dollar bill is very fitting. The "Eye of Providence", the all seeing eye on top of the pyramid, which is not only the Great Seal of the United States, but is also symbolic of the Illuminati. The Latin inscription, Annuit Coeptis, translates to "He approves of our undertakings" and Novus Ordo Seclorum is the "New order of the ages".

The future of money may be even more interesting than the past. With increased interest in a NAFTA currency, similar to the Euro zone, and now discussions of a global currency, further changes seem imminent. In fact, even now, we are being increasingly weaned from paper currency, to digitized currency. The use of electronic transfer, credit and debit cards, etc., has greatly reduced the need for paper currency. It may be possible some day that all transactions will be done electronically, by use of an implanted chip to record credit or debits to ones personal account. As fantastic as that may sound, the technology certainly exists today. Some believe that the RFID (Radio Frequency Implant Device) is in our future. This has led some critics to claim that the RFID represents the "Mark of the Beast", as referred to in biblical Revelations.

It's no wonder that after learning of the true intentions of the Federal Reserve System, President Woodrow Wilson, who signed off on the Federal Reserve Act, lamented: "We have come to be one of the worst ruled, one of the most completely controlled and dominated civilized governments in the world – no longer a government by free opinion, no longer a government by conviction or the vote of the majority, but a government by the opinion and the duress of small groups of dominant men."[7]

But this is just the beginning to understanding the old saying that "Money is the Root of all Evil."

---

[7] *Zeitgeist*, dir. Peter Joseph, by Peter Joseph, produced by Peter Joseph (United States, 2007).

Chapter 6 – Mind Control

While controlling money and economies are fundamental to those in power, the real key to maintaining power over people is the manipulation of the mind. If we look at our learning process from the beginning, we start with what we learn from our parents or guardians as our first teachers. They impart to us, from an early age, knowledge, beliefs, customs, morals, etc. If we then consider the trend that has been taking place for many years, there should be no doubt that parental influence is declining. Increasing financial pressures caused by inflation, along with increased materialistic pursuits, longer commutes, etc., have greatly diminished the family time required for this education process to take place. It is not unusual to hear people talk about "paying good money" in taxes or for private education to have someone else take responsibility for the education process of their children. At increasingly younger ages, children are shipped off to the care of others, often strangers, to begin the educational process, whether formal or informal. To make matters worse, there is increasing pressure within our society to have children enrolled in numerous organized group activities. The quality time between parents and children, or even for children to develop independent creative play, is minimal.

How did we get to this point? It is possible that we got here by design. In his video production "Freedom to Fascism", Aaron Russo provides a glimpse of how this has taken place. Russo, who asserts that through a friendship with one of the Rockefellers, was able to gain some insight into the activities of the global elitist operations in this country. While more of his findings will be discussed later, an interesting point with regard to the education phenomena, Russo claims that his Rockefeller friend informed him that the Women's Liberation movement was actually a creation of the elitists. The objective was to get women into the work force, with the benefits being two fold: to increase the federal income tax base (a tax that was implemented shortly after the formation of the Federal Reserve to pay interest on the money the Fed created), and secondly, to separate children from the home at an early age for "indoctrination" into the system. Others have echoed this same speculation, including leaked information the linked the CIA to the Women's Lib movement. Others alleged that Gloria Steinem admitted to funding for Ms Magazine from the CIA.

In looking at the formal public education process, we again see strong influence by the elitists. It has long been claimed that elitist groups are particularly well entrenched over the highest educational universities and scholastic publishers in the country. But aside from scholastics, public education is very much about socialization. Since the teaching of moral values, faith, and ethics are not part of public education, they have not gotten the attention they would have if more family time were available.

Aside from the lack of character building, another major inadequacy of our education system is in teaching critical thinking. Aside from what has already been said about the potential distortion of history, some believe education has by design, "boxed in the mind", or even "dumbed us down." The problem is that we do not learn to question "why" something happens. Take history as an example. We learn about people, dates, battles, etc., but rarely does anyone come away with a fundamental understanding as to why events take place. As an example, try asking someone about the cause of WWI. You will likely get something about the assassination of Archduke Ferdinand, or maybe something about the sinking of the Lusitania. But if you then probe deeper, as to what actually caused countries to engage in all out war, most really don't know. It is part of a "closed end" way of thinking that carries over to adulthood and obscures our view of current events.

We hear so much about the need to increasingly focus on math and science skills, but education needs to be much more than that. Complex thinking must include mastery of language, as thought processes are based on language. Highly developed languages, such as Greek or German, have produced leaders in philosophical thought. In today's pop culture driven, text messaging society, language skills and the complex thought process that they facilitate are failing. There is decreasing focus on the classical works that inspire artistic and literary appreciation. The ancient Greeks considered oratory arts, recitation and study of prose such as works from Homer, as elevating man to a higher existence. They considered such pursuits as what makes man more Godlike. A well rounded education must also include emphasis on literature, philosophy, the arts and history. It should inspire virtuosity, curiosity, rather than just providing enough knowledge to "run the machines and do the paperwork." This of course is not meant in a literal sense, rather, figuratively speaking.

One only has to look at the literature and philosophical thought of two centuries ago versus what comes out today to realize we are in retreat. While this is not to say we do not have astute thinkers and writers today, but one has to wonder why most people blindly accept increasingly difficult working environments, expanding governments, loss of liberties, large scale military actions and growth of the military industrial complex without even raising any questions. To a large extent, people have become completely complacent in their civic duty to challenge those in power because they are both unequipped or to busy to do so.

Influence of elitist thinking is particularly strong in secondary education. The development of the current global business environment would not have taken place without teaching MBA students the importance of producing goods in the most cost advantageous places. Globalism is probably the most emphasized and embraced business concept in any university business curriculum. However, we only learned the positive side of global business development. Many are beginning to wonder whether globalism has really been a positive development for the majority of individuals living in countries like the U.S., that have been ahead in terms of economic and industrial development. The movement of jobs and capital to other countries has created increased pressure on the U.S. worker, forcing them to compete with those in under developed countries. Huge trade imbalances add to the local economic woes.

The existence of elitist secret societies in universities such as Harvard and Yale including organizations such as the Skull and Bones, have long been the subject of many conspiracy theories. Many past U.S. presidents, political leaders, justices, military, and corporate leaders are connected in these elitist fraternities. The Yale influence goes beyond the U.S. borders, as former presidents of Mexico, Germany and the Philippines are alumni, as well as alleged connections between Chairman Mao Tse-tung of China and the University.[8]

Aside from our indoctrination through formal education, we can not ignore the tremendous contribution of the media to our brainwashing. Media "programming" may be an appropriate description of the deliverable. From the purchase of Reuters news agency by the Rothchilds at the end of the 1800's, to the purchase of

---

[8] Steven Sora : Secret Societies of America's Elite

Viacom by the Rockefellers, and overall consolidation of major papers and networks, media control is tightly held by few. Hollywood is also considered to be largely controlled by a small group of connected individuals. Television has become the most pervasive brainwashing device in history. Now in high definition, the images are "better than real." You can even select your flavor of the news, liberal or conservative…news to fit your own perspective.

In addition to controlling the news, the media keeps us entertained and distracted to such an extent, that we don't pay as much attention to the most important affairs of the state as we should. It is no wonder there is so much money involved in sports and the entertainment industry…it is key to keeping our minds occupied. But simply controlling the media and presenting biased information would be too transparent. The real key to successful manipulation of people's thinking can be explained using the philosophy of German philosopher Georg Wilhelm Friedrich Hegel. An "age of enlightenment" philosopher, Hegel proposed the Triadic concept, where:

Thesis + Antithesis → Synthesis

What this means in short is that two opposing actions result in combined overall result. For the purposes of controlling individuals, where you have two opposing perspectives, e.g., liberalism vs. conservatism, democrats vs. republicans, socialism vs. capitalism… if you control both inputs, you control the output. The secret behind the media now is that it controls both sides, so people believe they are choosing between different ideals, but both are ultimately controlled by the same people. Like the education process, you get into "closed end" thinking. For example, you might have two opposing views about the size of troop buildups in a conflict, but may not hear any view about why are we even in the conflict in the first place. At a high enough level, much of the political disputes we see are mere theater.

This is not to say everything reported in the media is fabricated. There are many professional journalists and most reporting is not deliberately meant to manipulate the reader or viewer. However, on key issues of national and international political and economic importance, one can assume that the messages conveyed to the public will be carefully controlled. As an example, if you consider the 2008 U.S. presidential election, the news coverage of the Obama / Clinton primary created hype that undoubtedly influenced the overall presidential outcome. On the other hand, political candidates with positions that were contrary to the controlling interests were ignored by the media. For example, candidate Ron Paul's platform was based on restoring liberties and scrutinizing the Federal Reserve role in controlling our monetary policy. However, because there was no public forum for these ideas, only those who knew where to find them on the Internet were aware these positions existed.

Another extreme example of media influence over the public followed the terrorist attacks of 9/11. It was impossible to turn to any news media without being exposed to the word "terror" over and over again. This occurred to the point where people were so "terrorized", they could not give up their personal freedoms fast enough. Terrorism can be substituted by something else, for example "economic crisis." If heard enough, this will create the appropriate fearful response bringing about the desired changes to business or financial systems all "for our own good". Undoubtedly, others will follow...perhaps pandemics or global environmental calamity. One must consider the link between the actual event, the expected reaction and the outcome...Thesis + Antithesis → Synthesis. The real indication that mind control is effective is when the target audience "insists" on the very actions intended by the creators of the message, but believes that they arrived at the decision independently.

Aside from the manipulations mentioned, the media has also played a destructive role in the societal values. Gratuitous sex and violence from Hollywood has pervaded our culture in such excess, that we are immune to any sensation from it. The portrayal of the religious as ignorant, even in cartoons, is unmistakable. The media has not only been destructive in the societal sense, but it is also used for character assassinations against anyone who speaks opposes those in control. Those who rock the boat usually end up as being some type of societal outcast. Some examples that come to mind, long time former FBI Director J. Edgar Hoover, a powerful insider with very strong Freemasonry connections (a 33rd degree "inner circle" Freemason himself) publicly admitted something to the effect that "there is a conspiracy so deep and so pervasive in this country, that even if the American public were to learn of it, they probably would not believe it." Perhaps it was this comment that caused the media exposure that led to his becoming known as a cross dressing, homosexual. The subtle character assassination of JFK as the philandering President is also more related to his politics rather than personal behavior. Countless others, including Hollywood actors and actresses, who speak out against conspiracies are labeled as lunatics, anti Semites, or whatever label that can be made to stick. In fact, if this book were to be successful, I would certainly expect to end up as some type of depraved, anti-American, terrorist, drug addict, etc.

Yet the most powerful mind control elements used today are related to nationalism, patriotism and heroism. Most Americans have, or should have, a healthy sense of American pride. There is much to be proud of, much to be grateful for. We owe tremendous debt to those who have given and continue to sacrifice so much, for others, particularly those who have served in our military. Even for those who have not served, almost everyone has family, friends, or someone close who has. The same holds true for law enforcement. Men and women, who served and continue to do so, act with selflessness and courage. In their hearts and minds, their actions are for the good of their fellow Americans. Continuous reminders in the media reinforce how police and military are the national heroes, but there is an unfortunate down side…the implied sense that anyone who disagrees with military or law enforcement doctrine is vilified. This is used as an extremely powerful tool to control anti-military or anti-terrorist sentiment. We have a very mistaken perception that patriotism means waving a flag, or putting yellow (made in China) magnetic ribbons on ones car, and blind obedience on military and homeland security issues. History has shown us many times that blind nationalism is dangerous to any society.

Finally, the mission of the media would not be complete without the occasional red herring…some story whose intent is merely to distract attention away from other matters, or to deliberately mislead the public into believing something that is not true. For example, one might get an overblown news story about some investigation of a CIA operation that gives the impression of a crack down on rogue operations. This gives the public some confidence that we, the public have some idea as to what is really going on within the CIA and everything is under control. This is likely a very false perception.

The role of the media should not be underestimated in its importance over public perception and support for elitist agendas. It gives us the enemies, fears, and distractions that are necessary to keep us off balance, under control, and to maintain the political-economic structure that keeps our leaders in power.

Chapter 7 – More on Politics

While I believe the majority of people entering the political arena are well intended, our current political system is easily corruptible. Starting with local politics, say any small or mid size town, appointments to public jobs for relatives or friends is pretty commonplace. Even granting contracts on small projects to friends or acquaintances can also take place without much notice. As you move up in size to larger cities, counties or state government agencies, these little favors, become bigger and more lucrative. As a lifelong resident of New Jersey, nicknamed the "Soprano State" due to its pervasive culture of corruption, I am all too aware of how the political payoffs system operates. Of course, the higher up you go on the political scale, the higher the stakes.

Washington is a pay for play city. Getting elected and maintaining political office takes money. Political Action Committees, or PACs, contribute to political campaigns to buy influence over the politicians they support. Large corporations access politicians through their employee PACs as follows: Employees are encouraged to make payroll deduction contributions, which might amount to say $1000/yr. In return, the PAC, through the company, provides travel and entertainment for the employee (and spouse) to PAC sponsored events that might be worth $2000/yr. This is the way companies circumvent the law that prevents direct contributions to a PAC. The company, through its employee's PAC, now has access to the politician, who can give serious consideration to the company's need for legislative action. The system works.

National politicians have control over the distribution of staggering amounts of wealth. The U.S. Office of Management and Budget posted figures (as of the writing of this book) showing federal receipts for fiscal year 2009 of $2.07 trillion, with expenditures of $3.56 trillion. One should pause for a moment at the enormity of these numbers, especially the $1.5 trillion of deficit expenditures. A rough breakdown on spending is 18% on pensions, 20% on health, 10% on welfare, 21% on defense, 31% on other. It's not hard to imagine that control over allocating these resources can certainly make politicians popular for those looking to feed at the trough.

But there is more to governing than being a rich uncle. The real power comes from being able to dictate domestic and foreign policy, controlling the world's most powerful military and having access to the best intelligence networks. This is why it is crucial for the real powers that operate behind the scenes to control the presidency and certain other key political positions. While most Americans find it easy to believe in corruption and election fraud in less developed or perhaps less sophisticated countries, they don't even fathom the possibility the same might be true here. Even in powerful nations, such as China and Russia, we have no problem accepting the existence of corruption at the highest levels of government. I recall attending a dinner where Garry Kasparov, former world chess champion, Russian political activist and presidential candidate was the keynote speaker. His emotion and intensity about corruption in Russian politics, where "election winners could be announced in the papers before the elections were even held," delighted the New York City crowd. I felt like I was probably alone in the audience of 1500, that believed we were probably not much different, other than the subtly of how politics are manipulated.

One of the most intriguing government operations is the CIA. I suppose most governments have some intelligence agencies, although there are only a few that are widely known within the U.S., such as the Brits with MI6, the Russian KGB, and the Israeli Mossad. The CIA connections, as well as British and Israeli intelligence operations run deep in the secret societies. First, it is surprising that the American public is so accepting that this organization operates in profound ways to protect the current power base in this country and abroad, with no accountability to the American people. We have come to believe, whether it is true or not, that the CIA is there to protect the American people from outside interests. We have a conditioned response to anything labeled "national security", giving it our full support, even though we have no clue as to what is really going on. On rare occasions we catch a glimpse of rogue CIA activities, for example, the Iran Contra affair, but it is what we don't know that is most intriguing. For example, in a later chapter, I will explore the cover up of covert Cold War operations as a possible basis for the 9/11 attacks.

The question we should be asking ourselves is who controls the CIA and whose interests does it really protect? For example, there is the alleged admission that CIA sponsored the women's liberation movement as discussed earlier. Perhaps this is true, perhaps not. One issue now accepted as factual, is that our CIA subverted the government of Iran in the 1950's at the urging of the British, to protect

British Petroleum from being nationalized by the Iranian government. The Brits gave us rationale to overthrow the government under the guise of potential Communist threat.   One could only imagine American resentment if we were to learn that a foreign government used clandestine operations to install their puppet government in the U.S. Yet most Americans don't seem to understand the anti-American sentiment that flows from Iran.

From time to time other stories are leaked about drug money flowing through the CIA to sponsor secret wars around the world, but in reality, we have very little knowledge about the workings of this organization or its British, Russian, and Israeli counterparts. Senate oversight does not provide a lot of confidence that they only act in the interests of the American public. I am a bit concerned about who is really in charge when I read a quote, "I couldn't get a job with the CIA today. I am not qualified." This quote was that of Congressman Porter Goss in a March 3, 2004 interview, about a year before becoming CIA Director.

Perhaps the CIA, or some rogue operation thereof, is responsible for a number of false flag operations that have pulled us in to many conflicts. As we start looking more closely, we see how misinformation is the key to conflicts throughout the world.

Chapter 8 – Wars and Other Conflicts

Having read quite a few historical accounts from different wars, it's hard to think of them in terms other than hell on earth. While sometimes glamorized in movies or expressed in terms of glorious achievement, I can't say that I have ever spoken with a combat veteran who didn't feel very strongly about avoiding wars except in the most dire of circumstances. Like most people, I personally know of those who paid the ultimate price of war and others who suffer life long ongoing trauma as a result of their service. Despite the well known horrors associated with war, the politics behind most conflicts are generally not well understood by the average person. The reality is that we don't know for sure whether or not our historical perspectives are very accurate. On the other hand, most people I know would rather go on believing that our nation has only engaged in wars based on the highest principles, rather than explore ulterior motives, even if they are true. Perhaps this has been the case throughout history, where both sides always think they are fighting the righteous battle. If we go back to accounts from the Old Testament, we find that sometimes God chooses the righteous side and leads them to destroy an evil enemy. On the other hand, we view some conquests, such as that of the Romans, the Ottomans, or the Mongols, as aggressive empire expansions. Yet, we see Anglo Colonialism in terms of "Manifest Destiny", or the "spread of democracy." That being the case, perhaps Attila the Hun was really an ideologist who was misunderstood by history.

Nationalism is largely responsible for conditioning us to think this way...that anyone who doesn't believe in the cause is anti-American. We have confused flag waving, jingoism, and yellow ribbons with patriotism, at the expense of virtue in truth. There are always two sides to any conflict, and as Winston Churchill so aptly stated, "The first casualty in any conflict is the truth." It would be interesting to see how the events of the past couple centuries are viewed five hundred years from now, particularly if changes in the geopolitical environment, such as the rise of China, changes the distribution of political power.

While not a historian, but having a higher than average interest in the subject, I have read my share of history and works of historical fiction. Again, I am not sure about the accuracy of what I have read, whether factual, deliberately misleading or unintentionally biased by the authors. As mentioned earlier, if you dig into more obscure sources, you find some very interesting and different perspectives on history, especially conflicts, from what is commonly accepted.

Starting with the American Revolution, we generally think of the founding fathers of this nation as strictly principled, morally uncorrupted, larger than life figures. The adaptation of our Constitution, which was based on the new enlightenment philosophy of the time, extended broad base rights to citizens well beyond what was available to citizens of most other countries. The ideals of new "God given" rights inspired a wave of revolutions in other European countries. However, not all historians believe that the American Revolution was solely based on this ideology, as some would say it was primarily sponsored by wealthy landowners and business people with the greatest amount to gain from independence with Britain. While from the British perspective, they were fighting to defeat piracy and illegal smuggling operations.

However, perhaps the most succinct explanation of the real cause of the Revolution came from Benjamin Franklin. Following the implementation of the Central Bank of England and their desire to control the currency of the colonies, this quote by Benjamin Franklin reveals the prevailing attitudes of the Founding Fathers: "The Refusal of King George III to allow the colonies to operate an honest money system, which freed the ordinary man from the clutches of the money manipulators was probably the prime cause of the Revolution."[9]

Despite motives for personal gain, it is easier to believe that the series of revolutions during the 1700's, beginning with the American Revolution, followed by others in Europe and South America, were ideological wars based on principles of enlightenment and their associated expanded rights. One would have a much more difficult argument to make with regard to the wars in the centuries to follow. Throughout the next centuries, wars appear much more of an asset grab, as colonial empires spread globally in a race to acquire resources and markets for their goods. For example, by the turn of the twentieth century, Britain had numerous territories throughout Africa, India,

---

[9] *Zeitgeist*, DVD, dir. Peter Joseph, by Peter Joseph, prod. Peter Joseph (United States, 2007).

Australia, Canada and parts of China.   British colonialism included such highly principled conflicts such as the Opium Wars in China, in which China sought to halt Britain's very profitable illicit drug trade (not unlike the present day wars in Afghanistan).   Similarly, nations including the U.S., Germany, France, Italy and Japan were seeking economic expansion and these imperialist nations carved up much of Africa, Asia and the Pacific Islands.   American colonies continued expansion here in North America against the American Indians as well as abroad.

In another example of what may be a case of "mistaken ideology", the American Civil War provides an interesting study. There were many underlying economic and State's rights issues putting the South at odds with the Union. By some historical accounts, slavery and man's right to live free were secondary issues. While it is hard to think of a more principled American figure than Abraham Lincoln, it was only after Lincoln learned about European interests to gain U.S. property by supporting the South, that Lincoln played the slavery card. His appeal to the people of Britain and France, worked to gain public support on higher moral ground, thereby thwarting the potential use of foreign troops against the Union.

Around the same period as the Civil War, there were revolutions and wars throughout much of Europe. In the mid 1800's, there were political upheavals in France, Austria, Hungary, Italy, and Germany. The Crimean War was being fought by British and French forces against the Russians over remnants of the Ottoman Empire. Some years later, more battles were taking place with unification in Italy and Germany.

In addition to Western wars, there were ongoing Asian conflicts, such as the Boxer Rebellion in China, a rebellion by some Chinese against Westerners and their influence in Peking.   The Rebellion was crushed by a military expedition of British, French, German, American, Japanese and Russian troops in 1900. In 1904, war between Russia and Japan broke out over control of Manchuria and Korea. In 1911, the Chinese Revolution ousted then Emperor T'ung, leading to the later face off between the Nationalists and Communists.

As previously mentioned, the economic and political rivalries that developed over the spread of colonial empires became more intense. Alliances were formed between those with strong economic and trading ties. This set the stage for the First World War, which was ignited by the assassination of Archduke Francis Ferdinand of Austria in June of 1914. The war would leave 10 million dead, 20 million wounded and lay waste to vast regions of Europe before ending in November of 1918 with the signing of the Treaty of Versailles.

However, the signing of the Treaty did not bring stability to the European continent. The crushing defeat of the Russian military by the Germans was followed by anti-government movements allegedly financed by powerful banking interests from England and the U.S. These powerful interests backed Leon Trotsky in an effort to overthrow the monarchy of Czar Nicholas II. Eventually, Stalin would oust Trotsky as an absolute dictator and purge Russia of all his enemies.

The unrests that followed the war were also responsible for the rise of another ruthless dictator, as Mussolini organized the Fascist party bringing it into power in Italy. The U.S. faced the Great Depression, which spread to other Western economies, furthering political turmoil and the rise of totalitarianism. Militarism was on the rise in Japan and power was consolidated under Prime Minister Tojo following the invasion of Manchuria, a territory of China. Civil war erupted in Spain, where Loyalists, backed by the U.S. and others, fought against the conservative Nationalists backed by Germany and Italy.

In Germany, harsh economic realities followed the large scale destruction that took place during WWI. Reparations imposed by the Treaty of Versailles, the printing of money to pay workers striking against the French occupied Ruhr, led to hyper inflation. The despair and economic turmoil gave rise to Hitler and the Nazi party. Under Hitler, the economy was directed toward building a powerful military machine, with the support of foreign bankers, including those from the U.S. and Britain.[10] With French and British consent, Hitler was able to annex Austria, followed by Czechoslovakia under the terms of the Munich Pact in 1938. Meanwhile, Italy having taken over Albania, now signed what was called The Pact of Steel with Germany and the Soviets agreed to a nonaggression pact with the Axis powers. With implicit and financial support from Allied powers, Hitler invaded Poland in 1939. However, the Allied powers would then turn against Hitler, thus igniting World War II. This conflict would claim more than 70 million lives before coming to an end in 1945.

As things grew worse for Hitler and the Axis powers, Hitler looked to take revenge against the financial powers who manipulated events that lead Germany into another disastrous war. He believed that the non-aggression treaties were a deception by the Allies to

---

[10] G. Edward Griffin, The Creature from Jekyll Island

manipulate Germany into expansion, giving them even greater control of territories with the defeat of Axis powers. He takes murderous revenge against innocent Jews, for the actions of the financial powers led by the Rothschilds and others.

The underlying causes in these World Wars were economic. Expansionism to increase territories, resources and trading alliances... all backed and financed by the monetary powers and all generating huge profits for suppliers to the war machine as well as huge profits on the repayment of national debt. It was all a very large scale gamble, with millions of serf lives lost in the wager.

When public support for the war cause was inadequate, the invisible hand would create events needed to bolster support. For example, in World War I, with the Allied forces struggling, the British ocean liner, The Lusitania, was purposely sailed into German U-Boat patrolled waters where it's sinking caused the death of almost 1200 of the almost 2000 civilians on board. The ship, technically an Armed Merchant Carrier, also carried ammunition, shell casings and other armaments as part of its cargo. Given that the ship would be delivering war supplies for the Allies, the German embassy publicly declared that the ship would be sunk if it were to sail in the war zones. It even tried to run ads in U.S. and other papers warning people not to be on this voyage, but almost all the major papers managed to not carry the warning. While the sinking did not directly result in the U.S. entering the war, it did turn the tide of public opinion in the U.S. and abroad. It was the financial interests backing the British and French, particularly J.P. Morgan and associates that finally persuaded the U.S. government to enter the war.

World War II provides another example of how the American public was manipulated into entering the war. With the Allied forces struggling and with U.S. neutrality, another event was needed to sway public opinion to support the U.S. declaration of war. The evidence of pre-existing knowledge by U.S. intelligence of the Japanese attack on Pearl Harbor is substantial and thus at least ten different inquiries were launched to determine what was really known in advance. Whether or not the exact time and nature of the attack was known, is still debatable. However, very few doubt that it was well understood at the highest levels in the government that the trade embargoes enacted against Japan would force an attack against the U.S.

Perhaps best said by the infamous Hermann Goering as he awaited trial at Nuremberg:

Steven Conrad

"Naturally, the common people don't want war; neither in Russia nor in England nor in America, nor for that matter in Germany. That is understood. But, after all, it is the leaders of the country who determine the policy and it is always a simple matter to drag the people along, whether it is a democracy or a fascist dictatorship or a Parliament or a Communist dictatorship. ...voice or no voice, the people can always be brought to the bidding of the leaders. That is easy. All you have to do is to tell them they are being attacked, and denounce the pacifists for lack of patriotism and exposing the country to danger. It works the same way in any country."[11]

The end of WWII would ring in a new era, not of peace, but of smaller scale wars, and other political actions to maintain control over what was now gained.

---

[11] Gilbert, G. (1995). *Nuremberg Diary*. New York: Da Capo Press. pp. 278–279. ISBN 0306806614. (From Wikipedia)

Chapter 9 – Who Needs Enemies?

The United Nations was established in October of 1945. Its' charter was to maintain international peace and security, and to promote international social and economic cooperation among nations. As the successor to the League of Nations, it had surpassed the earlier organization's accomplishments in terms of international economic development, but it failed to bring about a lasting international peace. The original charter of the U.N. was drafted in San Francisco by delegates from the U.S., Britain, China and Russia. The charter was later ratified by the five permanent Security Council members, which include those just mentioned, plus France. The charter espouses the same principles of human rights and freedoms that came out of the period of Enlightenment. In addition to this ideological component of the charter, there was the practical aspect of securing the peace and thus the spoils of victory won in the world wars. With this agreement in place, one might think the story could end here.

However, the New World Order had not yet been realized. There was still one important issue that remained unresolved…the underlying conflict between Western Capitalism and Communism. At the end of WWII, General Patton wanted to continue the march of U.S. forces into Russia, believing that conflict between the two countries was inevitable and that the U.S. would defeat the war battered Russian army in reasonably short order. Patton was denied permission to advance. The question then becomes, why? Conventional wisdom suggests that the war weary world needed to get on with peace and normalcy. But, there are other schools of thought on this matter. For example, some believe that despite the outward ideological differences, the same group of elitists, the people who engineered the Bolshevik Revolution, secretly control both sides. Others suggest that this same group decided on shared control between the East and West.

Given that the Russians and Chinese, the Americans and the Brits, were the four countries involved in the U.N. charter only to become the major adversaries behind the Communist and Capitalist political economic systems is puzzling. On the other hand, there was an important element missing from the U.N. charter that would maintain the current political stability and control: fear. Certainly, one could imagine the Cold War would fill that void. One might speculate that the true powers that operate invisibly set up different forms of government to see which form would ultimately be best for a global government... it is again, Thesis + Antithesis → Synthesis. There is the philosophical school of thought that man advances and creates only through conflict. Having competition, for economic and military superiority motivated by fear of the other side led to the development of military economic powerhouses of enormous proportions. The arms and space race with Russia, the economic race with China, has created incredible power for those in control. Further evidence to suggest that more takes place behind the scenes than commonly understood, is that Rockefeller (John D. Rockefeller III) could get an audience with the Kremlin at the height of the Cold War.

The next major conflict, the Korean War, would be a good test of the United Nations in resolving international conflict. The country was divided after WWII, with the Soviets controlling the North and the U.S. controlling the South (of course without any input from the Koreans). This resulted in continuous conflicts between the North and South, eventually escalating into civil war. The U.N. was called upon to intercede and with the Soviets abstaining by "boycotting" the vote, a resolution passed and the Security Council authorized a police action to resolve the conflict. The war that was fought to prevent the advance of Communism ended with very little change in the initial boundary between North and South. Casualties in the three year conflict vary, but most estimates put the number of total troops killed at over two million with civilian losses even higher.

Less than a decade later, the potential spread of Communism brought the U.S. into another Asian conflict, Vietnam. Following WWII, the French rulers in Indochina, were defeated in 1954 by the Vietnamese under Communist leader, Ho Chi Minh. Like Korea, the country was divided under the Geneva Convention with Soviet control to the North, and American control to the South. The conflict began for the U.S. under Kennedy, but with very limited military involvement. However, following Kennedy's assassination, a false flag operation, which claimed that U.S. warships engaged torpedo boats in the Gulf of Tonkin occurred. This led to the passing of the Gulf of Tonkin Resolution, which allowed the expansion of military operations without the declaration of war. The U.S. became embroiled in another long, costly war. Over 56,000 U.S. troops were among the 1.5 million soldiers plus 4.2 million civilian casualties that took place in Vietnam,

Cambodia, and Laos as a result of the conflict. The lack of understanding the nature of the enemy, and of our military objectives still haunts many today. The loss of life, over $100 billion in war expenses, and not really understanding what we were fighting for will not soon be forgotten by most Americans…or will it?

Some time in the mid 1960's, the government, whether the CIA or Department of Defense, commissioned a study on how to best create a stable society. A controversial and highly debated report that became known as The Report from Iron Mountain suggests the important role wars play in maintaining social order. While the authenticity of the study has been denied, such notables such as renowned economist John Kenneth Galbraith swear to its authenticity.

The full nature of the report has not been disclosed, but some general findings of the report concluded that war is a necessary element to a stable society. This is likely based on Freudian theories on innate human aggression. According to Freud, man is instinctively aggressive and restrictions on our instincts lead to unhappiness. Through socialization, we are able to accommodate some repression of this instinct as a tradeoff for security, i.e., longevity of life. "Loving thy neighbor" is possible if we can direct aggression toward a common enemy however, "loving thy enemy" stresses us to the fullest and is considered absurd by Freud.[12]

According to the findings, war fulfills the need for the military industry and the armed forces, extremely big business and employment provider for so many. It also provides outlets for society to direct aggression, which would otherwise turn inward on itself. There are suggestions that this theory is based on a natural human balance between good and evil. Some believe the report is merely a hoax, while others suggest that it is not only real, but was directed by top levels of government. Machiavellian in nature, the directive was to look at how to best keep secure the current form of governing rule, regardless of the human impact. War was only one option for the creation of outside enemies that was examined. According to now public sources, the study included the use of economic enemies, alien enemies, or blood sports as channels for societal aggression, thus directing attention away from the political leaders.

The question about the existence of aliens is always an interesting one. Numerous reported UFO sightings as well as the

---

[12] Freud, Sigmund. Civilization and its Discontents.

Roswell and Area 51 conspiracy theories create much speculation and controversy to this day. We have no way of knowing if there is more to the alien theories, or whether the sightings were really sightings of top secret government craft. There is still debate over whether or not the government was going to create an "alien" enemy for us...one that would galvanize and motivate us to increase our efforts to prepare our mutual defense against this potential enemy. Others, such as author Jim Maars, has suggested that understanding most of the mysteries of mankind, including the nature of man, who controls us and how, lies within this esoteric knowledge of aliens.[13] I will further elaborate on this later.

Whether aliens, Communists, terrorists, economic crises, or global warming, motivation by fear has become the common denominator for so many events that control our lives. This is the same today as it has been for many years.

---

[13] Maars : Rule by Secrecy

Chapter 10 – Current Political and Economic Issues

Despite the widespread "group think" influence created by the major news media, there are those outlying opinions on a variety of topical issues worth exploring. While it is difficult for most people to think outside the purview of the given "liberal" or "conservative" perspectives, these alternate views can be enlightening for the open-minded. The problem with outside the box thinking is that it usually invokes a conditioned response, be it dismissal, or sometimes outright hostility (as with the Allegory of the Cave). This is particularly true when it comes to issues that have been particularly engrained in our psyche, or where persons close to us have been directly affected.

To illustrate this point, perhaps it would be easiest to begin with a more benign topic, such as energy. Take for example the simple question, "is there an adequate supply of oil to last for say the next century", you will find expert opinions all over the map. In a conversation with someone from the US Department of Energy, I was told that the U.S. as well as other nations, "greatly over estimate reserves in information released to the public". This is done for "political reasons", presumably to keep prices of imported oil lower. Others have suggested that the U.S. has enough reserves to supply our needs for many decades to come, but we keep these reserves undeveloped so that we can tap into them when supplies around the globe become tight. It would seem the most likely reason for over stating reserves is that if people were to realize that reserves are short, hoarding would begin and energy prices would skyrocket. This would have a devastating effect on global economies, particularly high oil consuming ones, such as our own.

There is no way for the average person to know which scenario is true, if either. One has to wonder why we have only very recently begun giving serious consideration to alternative sources of energy, albeit, mostly driven by environmental concerns. For example, the U.S. the automobile industry looked like an arms race for decades, i.e., the bigger and more powerful, the better. In a sense, the public was "duped" into this arms race, believing they needed 7000 lb vehicles to keep us safe on the road, given that we were up against other 7000 lb vehicles. This of course, is somewhat exaggerated, by not entirely. But if one could take a step back and think a little outside the box, they would realize that if the objective is to move a 200lb person from point A to point B, do we really need vehicles weighing more than 2 or 3 tons, capable of speeds well in excess of 100 mph? This is especially true for commuters, who sit in bumper to bumper traffic in big, gas guzzling vehicles that might as well be dragging around giant anchors. Despite the prejudices against Smart Cars, minis, single occupancy vehicles, etc., if they were marketed properly, and the roadways were adjusted to separate them from trucks and full size vehicles, (similar to what has been done with HOV lanes), there is a tremendous upside benefit for the public. First, these vehicles could be mass produced at low cost to the consumer, they would be extremely fuel efficient or even battery powered, and they would significantly cut traffic congestion, meaning shorter commutes (2 highway lanes could equal 3 commuter vehicle lanes). Such a change could easily cut our national daily gas consumption in half from the current 350M gallons per day, as well as reducing CO_2 greenhouse gas emissions.

What makes this idea sound far fetched is the mindset to which we have been conditioned by good marketing. Had the auto manufacturers and energy companies promoted such an idea by marketing benefits to the consumer, with support from the government to make travel safe, the idea would not sound so ridiculous.

In a related topic, there is the debate on global climate change. Like many, I am a very strong advocate for protecting our environment, but am skeptical about global climate change based on burning of fossil fuels and production of greenhouse gases. The basis for my skepticism is not extremely scientific, although I have actually made my own calculations where I was able to determine an approximate atmospheric composition change based on the amount of fossils fuels burned globally and volume of the earth's atmosphere. Having some scientific background, knowing something about diffusion and other properties of gases, I believe that the very small compositional change in the make up of the atmosphere does not change the properties to the extent we would have global climate change. On the other hand, promoting global climate change may be a great way to change consumer energy consumption habits and bring about an evolution to alternate energy sources. It also is a powerful stimulus for development of new industries and associated economic growth. All that being said, the public is not in a position to know whether global warming is truly a threat, a means for collecting revenues on taxing greenhouse gases, or motivated by other political or economic reasons.

Despite the push for alternative energy sources, oil is still the life blood of the U.S. economic engine and of industrialized economies throughout the world. The geopolitical implications for oil producing regions are immense and again, some of the less publicized ideas on Middle Eastern politics are probably worth some mention.

For example, it is no longer a secret that the CIA organized a covert operation to overthrow the government of Iran in the 1950's under the pretense of preventing a Communist threat, when in fact, it was to prevent the nationalization of BP Oil. It would have looked bad for the Brits to organize this subversion, to protect a British company, but the secret alliances between those controlling both of our governments were obviously at work. If one needs to better understand the animosity between Iran and the U.S., just imagine for a moment how Americans would respond to finding out a foreign government used covert operations to overthrow our government in favor to one of their liking. (As far as we know, this has not yet happened).

While we tend to believe news reports that show a backward, American hating culture throughout much of the Mideast, one has to question whether we are seeing a true representation of the region. Undoubtedly there are many that believe Western nations, especially the U.S. have taken advantage of the oil producing nations by supporting oppressive regimes that control wealth very tightly, while their average citizen receives very little benefit from their country's tremendous natural resource. On the other hand, I believe most people there are not much different than most of us, who are primarily consumed with providing a decent life for themselves and their families. I can only speak from limited personal experience on this matter, but having worked for a non U.S. based international company, I have worked with people from both Iran and Iraq. From this limited exposure, I would be very hard pressed to identify any basic differences from typical Americans. In a conversation with an Iraqi engineer following the first Gulf War, he shared some of his perspectives, which he felt was typical of most....While Saddam Hussein was generally not well liked, the Iraqi society functioned in a relatively "normal" fashion. After the war, things got much worse, as they experienced significant shortages of basic needs, such as food and medicine. He said all he wanted, as did most Iraqis was decent "access to the necessities, food and medicine, and a chance for a better life for their children."

The economic sanctions imposed by the Clinton administration against Iraq, were blamed for the unnecessary deaths of 500,000 Iraqi children. In a *60 Minutes* interview with then Secretary of State Madeline Albright, her only response to this grim statistic was "it was worth it".[14]

In conversations I have had with a number of members from our military who have served in Iraq and Afghanistan, the perception seems to be the same. As one retired major put it to me, "I feel we are the world's bully." Further, he claimed that having served in both Iraq and Afghanistan that, "one thing is for certain... the people there pose absolutely no threat whatsoever to people in America." This is not an isolated opinion, as there are significant numbers of vets who believe our efforts in the region are either misguided or ill advised. Organizations such as Veterans for Peace are making an effort to expose the true costs of these conflicts to the people of these nations, to the service men and women who courageously serve, and to American society as well. Some statistics the group cites include:

Iraq and Afghanistan refugees account for half of all refugees worldwide

Over 1.3M Iraqis died as a result of the war.

Risk of violent death has increased in Iraq 50 fold since the invasion

One in eight Iraqi children died from disease or violence prior to their 5th birthday in 2005.

Over 5000 U.S, soldiers have died in Iraq and Afghanistan.

Veteran's Affairs Department backlog of unprocessed claims has reached the 1 million mark.

The combined financial cost of the Iraq and Afghanistan wars is estimated (as of July 2009) at $878 billion. The U.S. spends more taxpayer dollars on military spending then the rest of the world combined.[15]

---

[14] Ron Paul. The Revolution.
[15] Thomas Paine Chapter – Veterans for Peace

As with previous wars, most Americans, do not really understand the true need for these wars. The politicians try to connect the terrorist attacks of 9/11 with Islamic Fundamentalism and Taliban strongholds in Iraq and Afghanistan. On the other hand, none of the terrorists who were identified in these attacks were from either country. What is even more disturbing is that the groups we are fighting in Iraq and Afghanistan are the same ones that have been supported by the U.S. and Allies for so many years. The U.S. supplied billions to Al Qaeda and Taliban over the years against the Russians and now the same weapons we have financed are being used against our own troops. But there are other, much more disturbing explanations for our military involvement in the region. According to various Internet articles, control over Iraqi oil and Afghan opium provided the strong economic incentive for those who manipulate our politicians from behind the scenes. Whether fact or fiction, there are some compelling cases supporting this economic argument. Anecdotally, there can be no denying the enormity of heroine growth in the U.S. (and Russia) since the U.S. invasion of Afghanistan, which followed Taliban efforts to eradicate much of the opium crop going back to 2005.

Adding to Mideast turmoil are the ongoing battles between Israel and its Arab neighbors. One would need to be much more of a scholar than I to truly understand the historical nature of these conflicts, particularly given how religious beliefs factor in to the equation. While it is impossible to explain here in great detail, it is worth at least some attempt at historical perspective of Israel, the Jewish people and the regional conflicts.

The religious traditions and beliefs of Christians, Muslims and Jews all have ancient roots tied to the patriarch Abraham dating back to around 2000 B.C. Abraham is considered the father of the monotheistic religions and the father of Israel. According to scriptural passage from Genesis, God makes promises to Abraham:

The LORD had said to Abram, "Leave your country, your people and your father's household and go to the land I will show you. I will make you into a great nation and I will bless you; I will make your name great, and you will be a blessing. I will bless those who bless you, and whoever curses you I will curse; and all peoples on earth will be blessed through you."

– Genesis 12:1-3 (NIV)

The biblical land of Israel, or Promised Land, is the region which, according to scriptures, was granted by God to Abraham and the Hebrew patriarchs. Its borders are described in Genesis as well as later biblical chapters and include some lands of modern day Israel, Lebanon, Syria and Jordan. The land was settled by the Hebrews following their Exodus from Egypt around 1260 B.C. Under King David, the Hebrew tribes conquered the region and made Jerusalem their capital. The kingdom reached its height of power and prosperity under King Solomon, son of David around 950 B.C. However, the land was divided into two kingdoms following the death of Solomon and a rift over high taxes levied to maintain the opulent court.

Invading Assyrian and Babylonian armies in the next few centuries caused displacement of many Jews, despite having ruled for most of the first millennium. However, during the rule of the Roman Empire and following the failed revolt in A.D. 132, Jews were expelled completely from Jerusalem. The Jewish Diaspora continued for two millennia, with the land of Israel changing hands numerous times until finally becoming part of the Ottoman Empire up until the 20th century.

It was not until the late 1800's and early 1900's before there was an effort by both Jews and non-Jews to return the Jewish people to the Land of Zion. The Zionist movement was predominantly driven by forces in Britain, led by Baron Rothschild, as representative for the Jewish people and British Foreign Secretary Arthur James Balfour. The Balfour Declaration of 1917 established a policy of British support for the establishment of a Jewish homeland in the land of Palestine. Following World War I, the British Mandate of Palestine, drafted by Allied powers and approved by the League of Nations, gave Britain formal rule over Palestine from 1917 to 1948.

The plans to divide the Ottoman Empire, which had supported the Central Powers during the war, included granting the Arabs an independent state (UAE) in exchange for their Allied support during the war (through Lawrence of Arabia), establishing a home for the Jews in Palestine (through Baron Rothschild), and also giving the Hashemite family control over most of the remaining region for their financial support in the war. The Hashemite family, proclaimed descendants of the prophet Mohammed, were a very wealthy and powerful family. The family led a revolt against the Ottoman Empire in 1916, supported by the British, and firmly established control over much of the region. Following the War, different Hashemite family members established rule over areas of Jordan, Syria, and Iraq. With the establishment of the British Mandate, the remainder of the Ottoman Empire was to be displaced to Asia.

While so much more can be written about this region, it would require at least a book of its own.   The significance in terms of religious, political and economic impact is difficult to grasp.   Control over such significant oil reserves and the Holy Lands for more than half the World's faithful is of immense importance to the powerful.   But the region remains unstable, without true peace since the official establishment of the Jewish state in 1948.   A series of wars between Israelis and neighboring Arabs have occurred since the onset of statehood.   Due to the economic and religious significance of the region, it also is the epicenter for many controversial conspiracy theories.

Despite many tensions with the British during the Zionist movement and the establishment of the Israeli state, some suggest that Western motivations for supporting the Zionist movement were to create a regional ally in a region of major economic importance. With oil being the life-blood of Western economies, establishing a presence through a key ally was critical.   Others believe that religious motivations played a role, as the establishment of the Jewish people in the traditional land of Israel is part of the Christian eschatology. Others believe it was simply a repayment to the wealthy, whose strong financial support of the Allied war effort was critical.

Whatever the case, support of Israel and certain political leaders of "friendly" Arab states who are willing to work with the U.S. to supply oil, has had an after effect in the Muslim world.   Strong anti-West, especially anti-American sentiment has given rise to a new enemy – terrorism.

While most people in the World are content to go about their daily business, making the best of their lives, even when situations are very difficult.   In truth, we are all not that different and without outside influence could probably, at least reasonably, coexist peacefully. But there are always those whose motivations, whether idealistic or self-indulgent, will make enemies and manipulate others to join their cause.

Chapter 11 - 9/11, Terrorism and Aftermath

The conflicts of the World Wars have faded from the memories of most, as there are very few persons alive who actually lived during World War I, and even those who were old enough to either serve, or be directly affected by World War II are largely gone. Korea and Viet Nam are becoming more distant memories for all but the ones who were directly involved in a significant way. However, the events of 9/11/2001 remain indelible memories to almost everyone alive today. Thus, the subject is likely to draw a strong emotional response from any side someone takes on the issue. That having been said, I will nonetheless present various views to what remains a very controversial issue.

Of course we all know quite well that the World Trade towers were struck by hijacked commercial jetliners about 30 minutes apart on the morning of September 11, 2001. Unfortunately, this is where the agreement on what really happened and who was responsible, ends.

Like most Americans, I was stunned by the events of that day and in such disbelief, as it seemed so surreal. Like everyone else, I tuned into news coverage for days and weeks following the events, looking for answers and a better understanding. As details became more known, the evidence and the compelling links to terrorist cells seemed to fit together. However, in the years to follow, I have come upon alternate versions of this event. Reading various web site accounts, watching video accounts, such as Zeitgeist[16], and discussing with a wide variety of people, including some Washington insiders, an entirely different perspective emerged. While most believe that the accounts from the major media were in fact, accurate, having seen the other "conspiracy" side, I can no longer accept that something was not terribly afoul. Yet today, I hope that the public version of events from that infamous day are true, but unfortunately, I am not currently in a position to accept them. The following are some of the many alternate explanations of this infamous date.

---

[16] Zeitgeist – The Movie by Peter Joseph

Beginning with the date of the attacks, September 11th or 9/11, is considered by most Americans to have been selected in connection with 9-1-1 emergency services. This is a pretty absurd notion given the background of those responsible. On the other hand, September 11, 1683 represented a very significant date in the history of Christian and Muslim conflict. As Catholic apologist Hillaire Belloc wrote:

The last effort they made to destroy Christendom was contemporary with the end of the reign of Charles II in England and of his brother James and of the usurper William III. It failed during the last years of the seventeenth century, only just over two hundred years ago. Vienna, as we saw, was almost taken and only saved by the Christian army under the command of the King of Poland on a date that ought to be among the most famous in history-_September 11, 1683.[17]

Many questions also surround the perpetrators of the attacks. Beginning with the alleged mastermind, Al Qaeda leader Osama bin Laden, we need to understand a little history. The bin Laden family is a very wealthy, well connected Saudi family, with ties to Western business interests, including such notable corporations as The Carlyle Group. The Carlyle Group is a private equity investment firm with approximately $85 billion under management. Company holdings include everything from real estate, defense contractors, communications companies, as well as names such as Dunkin Donuts, and Hertz. The company has employed or has had as investors notables such as President George H. Bush, Secretary of State James Baker, British Prime Minister John Major, and George Soros.

While U.S. intelligence sources, both the FBI and CIA, believe bin Laden is the mastermind behind the 9/11 attacks, there remains controversy even over this point. There are accusations that the CIA had supported bin Laden and al Qaeda from the late 1980's until about 1990 in the Afghan fight against the Soviets. There are a number of claims that suggest he was even given dialysis in a U.S. military hospital in the 1990's.

There is also considerable controversy over the identities of the alleged hijackers. Reports from various media sources have claimed that several of the identified hijackers have come forth since the attacks, proclaiming their innocence, (which would seem to be substantiated in the fact that they are still alive). Many doubt that the

---

[17] Hillaire Belloc, The Great Heresies.

expertise needed to fly large commercial jetliners into their targets could be learned at the small aircraft aviation schools in Florida, as claimed in FBI reports. Then, there was the famous "passport" of one of the alleged terrorists found in the tower rubble. With the utter destruction and devastation that took place, fires allegedly hot enough to create molten steel, this passport miraculously survives?

There are a number of experts, including some from top universities, who feel certain that the fires generated by burning jet fuel could never reach temperatures high enough to create the molten metal flows described by so many firefighters in the aftermath. In addition, countless witnesses have described massive explosions before the towers collapsed. Evidence from main structural beams appeared to be cleaved by thermite, which would better explain the rivers of molten steel. Demolition experts claim that the way those buildings were dropped, is just how they would have taken them down if they did on purpose demolition. Adding to the speculation of conspiracy was the mysterious collapse of Building number 7, that came down in a similar manner despite not being hit by the jetliners or the associated fire. Some speculate that the destruction of Building 7 was symbolic mockery of the terrified people whose insignificant lives would be forever changed on that day.

The destruction at the Pentagon is also very controversial, as there are no public pictures or video of the jetliner crash. Any videos from nearby businesses, such as hotel security cameras, that may have captured some footage of an incoming jetliner were immediately confiscated and not released to the public due to "national security reasons". The rationale given was that they would reveal Pentagon defense systems. The controversy remains that the wreckage at the Pentagon site, as well as the site in Pennsylvania, are perhaps not consistent with jetliner wreckage. There are those who believe with a high level of certainty, that the Pentagon was hit by some type of missile.

Another point of controversy is whether or not our military was deliberately put into drills the morning of 9/11 that prevented them from scrambling fighters to intercept the hijacked jet liners. East Coast military exercises were taking place on that morning for readiness preparation of a terrorist attack using commercial jetliners.

One very interesting version on the 9/11 incident involves a CIA cover up of Cold War activities from a decade earlier. In a report titled : *Collateral Damage: U.S. Covert Operations and the Terrorist Attacks on September 11, 2001*, E.P. Heidner describes in detail the intricate plot to destroy records and a related investigation into illegal operations used in the dismantling of the former Soviet Union. According to the author, the CIA, engaged with other foreign governments and financial entities, put together an enormous monetary war chest, the primary source being enormous off the books gold that has been held by the CIA since its recovery from the Japanese following WWII. The story alleges a massive plan that involved insiders at the KGB and various Russian officials, as well as banks and financial entities, to facilitate the economic collapse that finally marked the end of the Soviet Union. The attacks, according to this article, were designed to destroy vital securities and records which would have linked $240 billion in funds to this covert operation. The targets, the Twin Towers, Building 7, and the Naval Investigative office in the Pentagon, were specifically selected based on the records they contained. The article details the key CIA operatives, links with Osama bin Laden and Mohammed Atta, the elitist bankers and the Federal Reserve. The conclusion of the report is that the loss of 2,993 lives was justified by the CIA as collateral damage to end the Cold War. [18]

Neither the American public, nor Congress really knows what led to the infamous attacks. In November of 2002, The 9/11 Commission was established to investigate and produce a comprehensive report on the entire events leading up to the attacks. The Commission was to determine how the attacks could have occurred and what should be done to prevent future attacks. Originally, President Bush wanted to appoint Henry Kissinger to lead the Commission, but Kissinger later resigned due to unwanted public disclosure issues. Former New Jersey governor Tom Kean took over as Commission chair and with the Commission's findings, comes strong evidence supporting a conspiracy.

First, President Bush and Vice President Dick Cheney refused to testify under oath to the Commission, as did their predecessors, President Bill Clinton and Vice President Al Gore. Bush and Cheney also would not agree to separate meetings with the Commission, only agreeing to interview together. From the onset, the Commission was under fire based on claims of impartiality and conflicts of interest. The "independence" of the Commission often came into question, and their reports indicated that Government Agencies, particularly the CIA were not only uncooperative, but even obstructed their work. Former

---

[18] http://www.scribd.com/doc/4866520/Collateral-Damage-911-Covert-Ops-Funding-Targeted

Governor Kean would later comment that the Commission was "set up to fail".

John Farmer, senior counsel to the Commission stated that the investigation "discovered that...what government and military officials had told Congress, the Commission, the media, and the public about who knew what when — was almost entirely, and inexplicably, untrue." Farmer continues: "At some level of the government, at some point in time ... there was a decision not to tell the truth about what happened...The (NORAD) tapes told a radically different story from what had been told to us and the public."[19] Thomas Kean, the head of the 9/11 Commission, concurred: "We to this day don't know why NORAD told us what they told us, it was just so far from the truth."[20]

At a Washington rally in July of 2008, I spoke with someone who claimed to have worked for the National Security Agency at the time of the attacks. He firmly believes that there was advanced knowledge of the attacks within the agency. He also claims the Israeli Mossad had advanced knowledge and there were Israeli agents present on 9/11.

Former Hollywood producer, the late Aaron Russo, provided some insight into the conspiratorial powers that operate in the U.S. and abroad. Russo, who claims to have been invited into the "ruling club" by friend Nick Rockefeller, discussed how the powers behind the scenes operate in his video "Freedom to Fascism". In his video Russo alleges in March of 2001, Nick Rockefeller told him something to the effect that "there will be terrorist attacks here in U.S. that will have our servicemen running around caves in Afghanistan looking for terrorists." When Russo responded in astonishment, saying that with all the money and power they (this ruling group) have, why would they do such things? The answer, according to Russo was, "Why do you care...they are just serfs anyway."

The aftermath of the attacks are far reaching...the tragic loss of life, the haunting images for the survivors, the subsequent wars abroad, and the loss of liberties at home. To the many who believe in the

---

[19] Eggen, Dan (2006-08-02). "9/11 Panel Suspected Deception by Pentagon". *The Washington Post*. http://www.washingtonpost.com/wp-dyn/content/article/2006/08/01/AR2006080101300.html. Retrieved 2009-05-31.(Wikipedia)

[20] Farmer, John (2009). *The Ground Truth: The Untold Story of America Under Attack on 9/11*. Riverhead Books. ISBN 1594488940. (Wikipedia)

conspiracy behind the attacks, they represent a major milestone in the advancement of the New World Order...the ultimate plan of global domination by the ruling elite. The attacks had all the tell tale signs of another false flag operation...the creation of an enemy and galvanization of the public in support of its destruction.

Outright military action in Iraq and Afghanistan were direct consequences of the terrorist attacks, despite no real link to the attacks themselves. None of the perpetrators identified with the attacks were Iraqis or Afghans. Further, alleged weapons of mass destruction in Iraq turned out not to exist. The death toll from these wars is well over a million and continues to grow daily, while countless others suffer from the ongoing realities of hunger, sickness, anarchy, and poverty. Some supporters of the invasions may maintain their beliefs that it was for the good of Iraqi and Afghan citizens...that the mistreatment of women and backward cultures needed to be defeated by the great liberators. Those same people should question why we were not guided by the same principled actions into far worse human crises in Africa. The answer should be obvious; there was no perceived gain for us.

The more subtle attack that followed 9/11 involved the liberties of American citizens. The prolonged effect of having "terror" drilled into the minds of the public had a profound effect on the American psyche. The once so highly cherished freedoms and liberties enjoyed in this country could not have been given up more easily. The true American spirit, which would never let the terrorists win by allowing our freedoms to be taken away, was drowned out by the media fear frenzy. It seemed that the public could not give up their freedoms fast enough to protect ourselves from the terrorists.

The formation of a Homeland Security czar, the militarization of police, and the suspension of Constitutional rights by the Patriot Act were all direct fallout from the attacks. Wire taps and arrests can now be made without due process. For people who see ulterior motives behind the terrorist attacks, the loss of liberties becomes even more profound and we have not likely seen the worst of it. The Real ID Act of 2005 set Federal Standards for state driver and identification cards, linking us to national databases. While the measure passed, many states did not comply as they viewed this as an unconstitutional breach of state authority. With a number of states pushing for resolutions to defeat the National ID requirement, there has been some backing off by federal officials. However, a new program was promoted by President Bush requiring health care federal IDs. There are even proponents of RFID chips inserted into all Americans as a way of tracking all of us, thereby being able to identify us from the terrorists. Perhaps many state drivers license are already encoded with some type electronic device that can be used as an electronic fingerprint of the holder. Taken to the extreme, the issuance of federal IDs as part of a larger, eventually global program to "chip" all of mankind leads some to the apocalyptic prediction from the book of Revelation, that the IDs represent the "Mark of the Beast." No one will be able to make purchases or sell anything without it.

Even our access to information on the Internet is being threatened. In a bill sponsored by Senator Jay Rockefeller, the government is looking to enact emergency powers to take over the Internet in the case of terror threat. One has to wonder what constitutes a terror threat...perhaps someone might be out there with the truth? This measure is probably not even necessary, considering no authority from Congress will actually be required to enact this into law. With the new found powers not authorized by the Constitution, the executive branch has been routinely exercising executive orders as a way of circumventing Congressional authority.

In addition to the attack on our liberties, there was also an attack on the American economy, as the hundreds of billions spent on homeland security and the nearly one trillion dollars for wars in Iraq and Afghanistan placed a substantial drain on economic resources that might otherwise be used to build productive capacity, or otherwise stimulate economic growth. One has to question whether it makes sense to spend hundreds of billions in security measures, while at the same time having basically open borders, with an estimated 30-40 million undocumented aliens entering the country during the period since the attacks. If the administration was really concerned about national security, would open borders not have to be considered a serious threat? On the other hand, the large influx of illegal aliens has provided justification to build massive internment camps throughout the country. Or, as discussed in the next chapter, perhaps economic destruction was actually part of the overall plan.

Chapter 12 – Economy in Crisis and Socialism

It should come as no surprise to find the U.S. economy in its current peril. The control over economic policy in the U.S. by the Federal Reserve and throughout much of the world by other central banks is in a sense, a con game. By using the tools at their disposal, the money printing presses, reserve rates, money supply, interest rates and inflation, the world bankers can finance militaries, national debts, trade deficits, etc. The politicians play their role in this arrangement, using money printed out of thin air to finance everything from military operations to social programs, keeping them popular with their constituents.

The con of course, comes at the expense of the saver, whose monetary assets erode as the true value of their savings is inflated away. On an international scale, the game becomes more complex, as currency valuations impact prices for commodities as evidenced by the run up of oil to levels in the $140/barrel range prior to the economic collapse. Gold prices have also soared from under $400/ounce to over $1000/ounce in just a couple years. The U.S. dollar weakness against the Euro and other foreign currencies at untested lows is another indication of potential problems brewing. Oil producing nations are now talking about abandoning the U.S. dollar in favor of more stable currencies.

But the biggest surprise about the recent global economic crash is how few "experts" predicted it. Even with a limited background in economics, I had been calling for the crash for at least two years before it happened. It was obvious that the normal economic cycles caused by Fed control of the money supply were not occurring. The continual pumping of liquidity into the markets with artificially low interest rates created soaring stock and asset valuations, particularly in the housing market. The government got into the act, by easing lending standards, and encouraging government backed agencies (Freddy Mac, and Fannie Mae) to make more credit available to those who probably could not really afford to buy. With real estate valuations sky rocketing, no one was worried about mortgage defaults. In the meantime, the banking geniuses figured out a way to package these bad mortgages into various types of financial instruments and derivatives for sale to unsuspecting investors. These gimmick instruments have been growing in popularity as great way to perplex investors and regulators behind more smoke and mirrors. Nevertheless, it is incredible that more experts were not aware of the bubbles being created, especially the likes of Fed Chairman Alan Greenspan and others.

But the economic attack on America has been taking place on several fronts. For all its alleged benefits, the nature of globalization creates something of a "leveling" effect in economies based on production costs. MBA schools have been touting the benefits of globalization and low cost production regions to legions of graduates who then go out to push manufacturing jobs to Asia. The low cost goods are then imported back in to the U.S., where we exchange them for U.S. debt securities. The trade deficit represents more debt for the U.S, but through inflation, much of the value of the debt can be inflated away. Having foreign countries finance our debt has some advantages, as the value of our currency depreciates, the prices of the imports do not always rise proportionately, so the differential is sometimes absorbed by the importer in terms of lower profits. In fact, unless the trading partner uses the U.S. dollars it obtains to purchase other goods, it has basically supplied us with usable items in exchange for worthless paper. On the other hand, our worthless paper subsidizes these foreign businesses and allows them to sell at artificially low prices, thereby driving out U.S. competition, so that they can then eventually raise prices dramatically.

According to the CIA World Factbook, the total foreign held U.S. debt exceeds $13 trillion dollars, with only Great Britain close behind at over $12 trillion. If the American debt holders or the oil producing companies decide to dump the dollar, a catastrophic collapse of the currency could trigger economic turmoil and hyper inflation in this country that would be unprecedented.

The amount of private and government debt seems to pile up without end. Just prior to the 2008 economic collapse, reports indicated that the savings rate in America was negative, i.e., more debt than savings. Many, if not the majority of Americans will be paying interest on loans and credit most, if not all of their lives. One might say that we, (like the Brits), are a nation enslaved by debt.

The real question becomes, does the system work, or when will the whole mess implode? There is considerable debate surrounding the global economic engineering that is being orchestrated by the world bankers and their political cronies. It really requires some dissection to understand the impact this globalization has on real people. There are really several components that need to be assessed, real wealth, productivity, and work/life balance.

First, if we look at wealth creation, it is hard to deny that capitalistic global economic structure has created incredible wealth for so many. People now have larger homes, full of great electronic gadgetry, big SUV's and some even have healthy 401k plans. However, if we consider the societal impact, there picture is not so bright.. Probably the most significant impact on real family wealth is more a function of dual income households and fewer children then global economic growth.

The great technology revolution that was to set us free from the burdens of labor has done anything but. We are so connected by computers, cell phones, and other hand held electronic devices that work has almost become 24/7. People are accessible any time of day or night, weekends and vacations…and it is becoming increasingly the norm to cut into what was previously personal time.

We have rid ourselves of many blue collar jobs, manufacturing jobs that a generation ago could have provided for a household even with 3 or 4 children. Increased productivity has eliminated many more jobs throughout many sectors of our economy. The standard 40 hour work week of no more than about two decades ago has routinely become a fifty to sixty hour work week for most professionals. Likewise, taking all entitled vacation days is rare. Give backs, in terms of pensions, health and other benefits have impacted the majority of white collar workers.   Job market shortages make the prospects of finding something better rather dismal.

The fall of organized labor, overseas job displacement, and increased productivity, has disproportionately benefitted the wealthy, especially the large corporate stock holders, while others are left hoping that their trickle down spending will generate enough job opportunities to sustain the masses.

Perhaps we can take solace in knowing that the movement of our jobs overseas greatly increases the standard of living in countries such as China and India. I can not say first hand whether or not this is true, but time will tell whether they fall into the same situation we face here, i.e., cheaper goods can be produced elsewhere and they find themselves working harder and harder to try and maintain what they have gained over the years. We frantically compete educationally in a global environment, not to fall behind others in math and science, lest we find ourselves without the all important technology jobs of the future. The truth is that the majority of the globe has become nothing more than commodity labor for the benefit of the elite. The illusion of financial progress is mainly that…an illusion. Increases in wages are largely off set by inflation. The improvement in technology and design of the goods we produce make it seem like we are getting ahead, but in reality, there just is not that much progress. If we really look at what has raised the aggregate standard of living throughout the world, it has been the creativity and labor of the people. Unfortunately, we are all manipulated by money, which allows the elite to manipulate and control all that is being created.

Having witnessed the decline of the blue collar or union class, we are now seeing a similar decline taking place with white collar workers. It seems likely that the next demographic to fall will be the upper middle class, or pseudo wealthy. Decimated stock portfolios, real estate holdings, looming inflation and the likelihood of a higher tax burden should help relieve this class of much of their wealth. They too will likely feel the squeeze with the loss of high paying executive jobs. The continued loss of real wealth could be a catalyst making the U.S. rife for dramatic socialist change.

While socialism has long been despised in the U.S., we have born witness to such high profile avarice and corruption in the last decade from unbridled capitalism that the public has become more open to government remedy. When we read that the top 20 hedge fund managers in 2007 earned an average of over $650M, when we think about Enron or Bernie Madoff, we think of capitalism run amuck. Place a well contrived economic crisis on top of everything else, and a total socialist revolution almost seems like it should be a slam dunk.

"Change", the mantra of the 2008 Presidential election, suggests that the nation is ready to move forward, in a new direction. Like so many contrived events in the past, those who created the crisis, will show us the way out. The economic crisis of 2008 called for drastic measures, at least that is what we are to believe. The hundreds of billions in taxpayer money used to bail out the irresponsible corporations on top of billions in economic stimulus, billions in very questionable foreign wars certainly causes more than just conspiracy theorists take pause. Many are sensing that there is a high degree of planning that took place to get us to this point. This new business government alliance has the President of the United States managing corporations such as GM and actually firing its president! While people applaud the government intervention to stop the payout of bonuses for employees of bailed out firms, they should also be wary of the implications.

Furthering the socialist agenda, the full court press is now on for some form of socialized health care. The President is insisting it is a "must have" for this country to avert future economic calamity. Why this is the case now as opposed to our entire historical past is not clear, other than as long as the government is spending trillions of dollars that we don't have, why not another trillion?

The question remains, what is the real driving force behind the socialist change? One explanation is that capitalism has run its course and is no longer viable as a political economy. We have had a good run with it over the last couple centuries, but in recent decades, it required trillions of dollars of debt to continue to function. In the absence of major structural societal changes, such as a strong rebound in population growth or some very revolutionary technological development, the old capitalist system, built on ever increasing growth, may not provide enough jobs to sustain the masses. With unemployment now approaching 10%, it may be time for a change.

On the other had, maybe the goal is quite different. Some believe that the real goal is bankrupting the nation and collapsing the currency. This will force a "global" economic solution, beginning with a global currency, (the idea of which has already been floated by Russia and China). Without the destruction of the U.S. economy, we would have no incentive to join the global plan. Others suggest that the various economic structures that have been established around the globe, capitalist, socialist, communist, etc., were done so as experiments, to see what functions the best. The theory being, that the global elitists who manipulate the governments of the world have selected something other than liaise faire capitalism for the New World Order. Those promoting this theory believe the present Chinese political economic model, which gives government a very strong hand not only in business, but also wealth distribution and population control, has been selected by the ruling elite..

In the Russian newspaper, Pravda, Stanislaw Mishin wrote an interesting article about American capitalism "gone without a whimper". In it he describes the difference between the bloody Russian struggles against the Wall Street backed Marxists, versus the American passive acceptance created by a psychologically defeated populace. He points to pervasive flaws in the education system, sell outs by the churches to the politicians, and in particular the changes taking place under the Obama administration. Mishin states that the hundreds of billions used to bail out the corporate thieves, makes the Russian oligarchs "look little more than ordinary street thugs, in comparison". He goes on further to describe his shock over a U.S. President taking control of the automotive industry and a Congress that will decide on proper compensation packages for employees of companies receiving any type of government money or incentives. He ends with a warning, coming from 70 years of disastrous experience, saying "The proud American will go down into his slavery with out a fight, beating his chest and proclaiming to the world how free he really is. The world will only snicker."

If you think that maybe things can only get better, think again. If you look at historical economic turmoil similar to what we face today in the U.S. and throughout the world, the possibility for economic crisis that ends in war becomes increasingly likely. For example, there are many parallels between Germany in the post World War I era and the U.S. today. Crushing debt, followed by hyperinflation, put the Germans on the path toward war. With some of our allies, such as Britain facing an even greater debt crisis than us, the only path to debt elimination may be war.

Perhaps that is the plan...we have been exchanging useful goods from China and elsewhere in exchange for digits and paper, meaningless IOU's. Maybe it won't matter.

Chapter 13 – Who is in Control?

Based on our understanding of history, the ruling structure of past ages seems quite clear. Be it kings, queens, emperors, pharaohs, or clergy, it was apparent who was in charge. But today, under the veil of secrecy, it becomes much less obvious. The real power is not with the politicians who come and go, but rather those who put them in place and pull their strings. There are many theories on who are these real powers behind the scenes. Some theorists focus on elitist secret societies such as the Skull and Bones, Fabians, Illuminati, Freemasons, or the Bilderbergs. Others, citing more traditional ecclesiastic power, believe that our real handlers are part of some clandestine religious group, be it Protestant, Catholic, or Jewish. Still others believe that a few families control most of the worlds' resources.

It is interesting to look at some of these theories, as incorrect as they may be. Beginning with the religiously oriented power structure, the first on many lists are clandestine elitist Protestants. This obviously derives from the traditional WASP (White Anglo-Saxon Protestants) control of major corporations and of course the highest political positions in the U.S. and Britain, the two major powers believed to be behind the New World Order. The wealthy and powerful in the U.S. from the origins of this country, the Astors, Rockefellers, Morgans, etc., were of this ilk. The term "Protestant work ethic" was made popular following the incredible success and wealth created by the likes of these families. In fact, John Rockefeller claimed that it was God who wanted him to achieve the success that he did, because of his work ethic. The fact that all of the U.S. presidents, except Kennedy claimed Protestantism as their faith helps reinforce this popular theory.

The Catholics were often targets of conspiratorial claims, this stemming from the long reign of the church over resources, politics and education, particularly in Europe. The Catholic Church has been historically criticized for suppressing thought that was contrary to its teaching, or as some suggest, threatening to its preeminence. There are claims that some Catholic orders, including the Jesuits, were very adept at mass mind control. Some suggest there is not only a Pope, but an

Anti-Pope, who is behind much of the political manipulation taking place around the world.

The Jews also get credited as the potential secret force behind world domination. Historically considered by the Abrahamic faiths as "God's chosen people", the Jews are considered to be a very powerful and influential group, particularly considering the relative small population versus Catholics and Protestants. There is the perception of very strong Jewish influence in financial institutions and media. This, coupled with the incredible financial and political dominance of the Rothschilds, puts secret Jewish groups high on the list of potential global domination conspirators. Some suggest that the sensitivity around anti-Semitism actually provides good cover for Jews to exercise political and financial domination. The Israeli Mossad has a reputation of being extremely proficient at covert operations, very much like the CIA. Perhaps more disturbing is the secret Mossad motto: "By way of deception, Thou shalt do war".[21]

While history suggests a connection between religion and the abuse of power, it is individuals and powerful families, not religions, who are corrupted. Throughout history, there have been arranged marriages of royalty and powerful families as a means of retaining and expanding power. While there may be some misguided distortion of moral authority connected with one's faith, one would be hard pressed to make the argument that the faith itself espouses worldly domination as its primary goal. Speaking from personal experience, of those who I know belonging to any of these religions, I feel quite certain that none are involved in any plot to control the globe for their faith.

Nevertheless, there are unquestionably those whose agenda is the promotion of a global government or global systems of control. Those who publicly promote the New World Order can cite highly principled reasons why it is so important. For example, the United Nations, set up after World War II as the successor to the failed League of Nations, was chartered to promote world peace by facilitating global resolutions to conflicts, economic development, human rights, and enforcement of international law. Despite such principled goals, the impartiality and effectiveness of the organization is widely criticized. Many believe that the true motivation for its establishment was to protect the status quo, which greatly favored the elitists with their substantial gains following World War II.

---

[21] Synagogue of Satan. Andrew Hitchcock p.161.

The IMF and World Bank are examples of the controversial agenda promoted by the U.N. Formed out of the Bretton Woods Monetary Conference in 1944, the chief architects were known socialist and communist party members. While chartered to help stimulate economic development in under developed nations, the real impact on nations receiving assistance is debatable. Aside from controversy over well connected bank presidents to politicians, the effectiveness of the organization has been called into question by such notable economists as Joseph Stiglitz. Incorrect implementation of World Bank loan agreements have been criticized as doing more harm than good. Critics site the Western imperialistic approach to funding under developed countries as having many strings attached. Part of the role of the Bank is to provide "teaching" and governance to developing countries. Others have suggested that the loans often benefit those in power, while having little or no positive benefit on the public, but leaving them further in debt.

In addition to the World Bank/IMF, there are other organizations that are not under the auspices of the U.N. but are designed to promote the globalist agenda. For example, Council for Foreign Relations is an American think tank organization established in the early 1920's by American elitists, many of the same people, who under Woodrow Wilson helped to create the Federal Reserve. The original charter under Wilson was to utilize a brain trust consisting of academia, corporate interests, journalists, CIA members, and high ranking politicians to develop post war (WWI) plans to stabilize the global environment.

Since its inception, the CFR has remained an important consultative service on foreign policy. Past members reads like a who's who in politics, including former Presidents George H.W. Bush and Bill Clinton, along with Dick Cheney, Dianne Feinstein, Alan Greenspan, and numerous notable others. Corporate sponsors include a list of many of the top multinational corporations in the world. While some policy papers generated by the CFR may be made public, its work is generally confidential. The group is also closely aligned with the Rockefeller, Ford and Carnegie Foundations. While much of the work remains secretive, the CFR is credited with developing foreign policy on Soviet containment, NATO, Viet Nam, the Marshal Plan and the opening and normalized relations with China.

In 2008, the CFR began a plan called "International Institutions and Global Governance: World Order in the 21st Century" which aims to set up global institutions to foster global governance and to tackle different trans-national problems:

Countering Transnational Threats, including terrorism, proliferation of WMD, and infectious disease

Protecting the Environment and Promoting Energy Security
Managing the Global Economy

Preventing and Responding to Violent Conflict

President Obama has pushed for U.N. support of the CFR plan.

As an off shoot to the CFR, then Chairman David Rockefeller formed the Trilateral Commission in 1972. Other co-founders of the organization included former Fed chairmen Paul Volker and Alan Greenspan. The scope of activities governed by the organization was to cover the U.S., Europe, and Japan. Membership in this organization is more global in nature than the CFR, but from the American side, has the same elitist members such as Clinton, Bush Sr., Carter, etc.

A Trilateral Commission Task Force Report, presented at the 1975 meeting in Kyoto, Japan, called An Outline for Remaking World Trade and Finance, said: "Close Trilateral cooperation in keeping the peace, in managing the world economy, and in fostering economic development and in alleviating world poverty, will improve the chances of a smooth and peaceful evolution of the global system." Another Commission document read:

"The overriding goal is to make the world safe for interdependence by protecting the benefits which it provides for each country against external and internal threats which will constantly emerge from those willing to pay a price for more national autonomy. This may sometimes require slowing the pace at which interdependence proceeds, and checking some aspects of it. More frequently however, it will call for checking the intrusion of national government into the international exchange of both economic and non-economic goods."[22]

Sen. Barry Goldwater wrote in his book *With No Apologies*: "In my view, the Trilateral Commission represents a skillful, coordinated effort to seize control and consolidate the four centers of power:

---

[22] Wikpedia.

political, monetary, intellectual, and ecclesiastical. All this is to be done in the interest of creating a more peaceful, more productive world community. What the Trilateralists truly intend is the creation of a worldwide economic power superior to the political governments of the nation-states involved. They believe the abundant materialism they propose to create will overwhelm existing differences. As managers and creators of the system they will rule the future."[23]

The points made by Goldwater are the crux to understanding how this group operates. This precept is simple…manipulate the masses with materialism to the point people will give up all else, including freedom and faith. The attacks that have taken place on religion are fundamental to implementing New World Order goals. This is probably most true for fundamentalist religions and may provide a reasonable explanation for the all out attack on Islam. There is no room for Iraq, Afghanistan, or Iran in the NWO unless they can conform to this materialistic ideology, give up fundamentalism and install a good central banking authority to over see the evolution. This is at least a more plausible an explanation than the one given to us by President Bush, who claimed we must take the war to these terrorists who attacked us because they were "jealous of our freedom". Can we really imagine people half a world away, dirt poor farmers and goat herders who probably could not find the U.S. on a map, plotting to destroy us simply because they heard we are free?

There is yet another more secretive elitist international group that factor heavily into the international political and economic scene. The Bilderbergers as they are now known, were formed in 1954, its name derived from the Dutch hotel where the first meeting was held. The group allegedly consists of 100 – 150 of the top global titans of business and politics. In addition to the usual cast of American characters, e.g., Bill Clinton, Timothy Geitner, Paul Volcker, Condaleezza Rice, Donald Rumsfeld, Henry Kissinger, David Rockefeller, it also includes the likes of Tony Blair, King Juan Carlos of Spain, Queen Beatrix of the Netherlands, top officials from BP, IBM, Barclays, the Bank of England, etc. These are only those who were listed publicly in the main stream press (source: Newark Star Ledger, March 17, 2009). This group is less public then either the Trilateral Commission or CFR, with its membership and meeting topics completely closed to the press. There is a loosely defined mission of the group, to create "a better understanding of the complex forces and

---

[23] Ibid.

major trends affecting Western nations." Some have suggested that it is within this group that our presidential candidates are selected. The primary topic of the referenced Star Ledger article was to discuss the close Obama connections with various Bilderbergers.

It is unfortunate that so many in this country were deceived into seeing Obama as being different, the face of change for this country. This could not be further from the truth, for he is, like his predecessors, a figure head controlled by the same forces. His public appeal, mixed racial, mixed religious background, youth, energy and ability to articulate positions made him a good selection for us, even though people did not really know much about his origins. The point being, he was the anointed messenger sent to bring socialistic change to this country. Probably the most honest and telling speech made during his campaign that revealed his true character was when he commented about "people clinging to their guns and religion" as being what ails this country.

Unfortunately, we Americans, like I our counterparts in the U.K. and elsewhere, believe that choosing a President is the public's choice. We do not really consider that we are given a very short list of "approved" candidates, and any outsiders are generally ignored by the media to the extent they become non-factors. One could clearly see this in the past election, where it was going to either be a Clinton, Obama, or long shot, McCain in the White House. Candidates such as Congressman Ron Paul, whose message about restoring freedom, the Constitution and sound monetary policy was very well received by those who heard it. Unfortunately, that was a very small group, as the media ignored him. It was only those who knew where to look for information on the internet understood what his campaign was about.

Then there is always the possibility of a President who falls out of line. For many years, there has been speculation surrounding the Kennedy Presidency and stories about his assassination. Unfortunately, we will probably never know the truth. However, it was well known that Kennedy was considered an "outsider" by the New York elite given his Irish Catholic roots. It is also known that a strong rift developed between Kennedy and the powerful elitists over a number of issues, including Kennedy's threat for an executive order to cancel interest payments to the Federal Reserve. Just prior to his assassination, Kennedy made a public address (that is available on the Internet) speaking out against the ruling secret society and threatening to expose it. According to the wife of accused assassin Lee Harvey Oswald, "the answer to the Kennedy assassination is with the Federal

Reserve Bank. Don't underestimate that....The people who supply the money are above the CIA."[24] Still, a number of other sources claim that it was the CIA under the direction of Howard Hunt and then Vice President Lyndon Johnson who orchestrated the assassination.

Aside from possible presidential assassinations, there are stories of activities within the secret elitist circle are very bazaar. "Inside Bohemian Grove" was a documentary of a men's only elitist group meeting that takes place in a remote area outside of San Francisco, known as Bohemian Grove. The Bohemian Club was formed back in the late 1800's as a place for drinking and festivities for prominent men. The tradition grew and continued to where it is now the preeminent spot for the world's most powerful men to go on a retreat of sorts. The objective is not to conduct business, although, the Manhattan Project was reportedly kicked off there in 1942, but rather to drink, enjoy plays and unusual rituals. Reports from inside have been disputed by attendees, who include many past Presidents, such as Nixon, Reagan, Henry Kissinger, as well as presidents of some of the largest corporations and prestigious academic institutions. Perhaps it is all in good fun, but the insiders have reported homosexual behavior and bazaar ritualistic plays and ceremonies including the burning of human effigies at the altar of a 40 foot owl statue. The symbolic ceremonies are supposedly cathartic in nature, but resemble satanic ritual.

The fact remains, that these aforementioned groups are all real and all work toward the same goal of global control. As with any such organizations, there is a hierarchy, or perhaps a true inner circle at the top of the elite. It is here, the one or few who control these elitist groups and in turn control presidents, world political leaders, central banks, intelligence agencies, and armies that one would find the true philosopher kings, the inner circle Illumanati, or whatever one wants to call them. The reason for secrecy is simple...If things go bad, you can replace the front governments without changing the real power. This provides global stability, continuity, and prevents anarchy. National and international security is paramount for those in control to stay in control.

---

[24]Maars, Rule By Secrecy, p 131

Chapter 14 - Religious and Philosophical Views

For thousands of years, man has tried to understand his role in this world, whether or not we serve a larger purpose, the nature of God, and what is truth. Human history is full of philosophical and religious views on rulers and the ruled. In this way, we are no different today than from any other period in history. On the other hand, the secret, deceptive nature, the technological and global reach of those in power today may set this period apart from any other in human history. The establishment of an elitist secret "government" controlling the world, while seemingly far fetched, raises very interesting philosophical and religious questions. Its reach goes beyond controlling economies, governments, armies, and media. As Barry Goldwater stated, control also includes intellectual and ecclesiastical aspects of humanity. This leads to some very interesting philosophical insights and opinions about the true nature of this power over humanity.

Reflecting back to the beginning of the book, where one considers the origin of the universe and man's place in it, certainly perspective on who rules lies in one's fundamental beliefs. For the Darwinist, including the majority of Enlightenment thinkers who view man only in terms of the physical world, as the coincidental result of the random combinations of carbon, oxygen and nitrogen atoms, the evolution of power may be answered rather easily. Those in control are there simply based on evolutionary advancement. In a sense it is survival of the fittest…being a little smarter and cleverer than the next person and utilizing these abilities to control and manipulate their given situation to their advantage. By this view, the evolution of a natural hierarchal system seems normal and quite acceptable. Conquest, wars over resources, particularly if you can get someone else to do the fighting, may come without much remorse. To the victor goes the spoils, to the defeated, their mission on earth, to convert food products and oxygen to waste and carbon dioxide, is completed.

Of course, this is not to say that the Darwinist, atheist or agnostic truly feels this way. Most still have a sense of what is right and wrong, moral and immoral, etc., even if they believe we are "just carbon." Whether a person is religious or not, there is still a general sense of right and wrong, good and evil, self serving or righteous. There is much in the way of individualist and collectivist philosophical thought governing who and how one should rule for atheists.   For example, there are philosophical principles of governance based on the collective or greatest good in society, independent of any religious beliefs.   Within these circles, science generally plays a key role and may even be viewed as the most important element of humanity, since it can provide the solutions to the physical problems in the world. However, without a source of moral authority, there is nothing to prevent selfish interests from replacing those of society.

The majority of the world's population believes that there is more to human existence, a metaphysical, spiritual, or however you want to state it that defines our essence and sets humanity apart from the rest of the species. This of course, is supported by the majority of the world population's belief in God as the supreme ruler over all. The human experience for those is defined by both physical and spiritual, and is defined in terms of good and evil.

Whether or not the present day "secret kings" are benevolent masters or self serving slave masters really depends on one's perspective. For many Americans, especially those living the so called American Dream, it is difficult to think of our leaders as being corrupt or evil. The tremendous wealth that has been created and the high standard of living enjoyed by so many is mistakenly credited to leadership that has our best interests in mind. The confusion comes with equating prosperity to "the good". By inference, the global socialistic society that provides the greatest economic benefit to the highest number of people might also be viewed as "the good". This is the driving philosophical thought behind the Fabian founders of the World Bank.

The notion of "the good" is not universally accepted. As outlined earlier, there have been numerous connections between the elitist secret societies and Satanism. Within these circles, there are those who believe Lucifer is "the good" the "Son of the Morning" who provides mankind with the heavenly knowledge to set him free from an angry and punishing God. Notions that the Church promotes darkness and ignorance while modern man with his scientific knowledge provides enlightenment have been popularized in modern culture. Dan Brown's Angels and Demons is a perfect example of Church deception working against the truth of science. On the other hand, some would argue that science is now master over us, as opposed to us controlling it.

Modern secularism has had very destructive consequences for traditional religions. There are some interesting but disturbing perspectives on these consequences. While most religions tend to avoid issues of political nature, there are some very strong, although sometimes veiled, warnings about what may be to come. Apocalyptic predictions are growing in number and vociferousness. The eschatological implications of the New World Order are quite profound.

While it is not my intent to cover in detail the eschatological views held by Christians, Muslims, Jews and Hindus, there are some interesting connections between the current events taking place with the establishment of the New World Order and beliefs relating to the conclusion of human history. Some see these events as foretelling signs predicted by scriptures.

For those not familiar with the eschatology, it is the area of theology dealing with the final events of the world, the final judgment and the fulfillment of God's ultimate plan for humankind. Christian eschatology is based on certain books of the Bible, particularly the Old Testament book of Daniel and Revelations to John in the New Testament. In short, it describes the coming apocalypse, the final judgment of the living and the dead, the second coming of Christ and the establishment of the heavenly kingdom here on Earth following the destruction of Satan in the battle of Armageddon. According to scripture, each of us will be judged based on our relationship with God and our deeds toward others on Earth. Just as there are considerable differences among Christian faiths on the treatment of death, i.e., when a soul reaches heaven or hell, or whether it remains for a period in purgatory, there are also many interpretations on the events leading to the Christ's Second Coming. These vary from those who believe it has already come as in a "spiritual" rather than physical sense, to others who have made incorrect predictions, and still others that believe the events are yet to come.

One of the more controversial views on the Second Coming has to do with dispensationalist belief. This is a scriptural interpretation that Christ will come to reign over the land of Israel, after the descendants of the biblical land of Israel have been returned and peace has been established. Some believe that this interpretation drives U.S. foreign policy to aggressively support Zionism and destruction of any enemies of the Zionist state. Some believe that Mideast politics may be driven more by eschatological beliefs than oil. Within this school of thought some suggest that the U.S. has not adopted energy conservation measures, alternative energy sources, or domestic reserves so as to maintain a strategic dependence on Mideast oil, thereby justifying our military presence.

While this idea seems a stretch, there are very strong indications that religious beliefs play a role in Mideast politics. Former French President Jacques Chirac revealed in an interview that President George Bush asked him for support in the invasion of Iraq in 2003 claiming "Gog and Magog are at work in the Middle East", "The biblical prophecies are being fulfilled", and "This confrontation is willed by God, who wants to use this conflict to erase his people's enemies before a New Age begins." The first American newspaper to report this story was the Charlestown West Virginia Gazette.[25] The reference to Gog and Magog, Biblical but somewhat nebulous enemies of God, is rather puzzling. Either this statement is in fact an indication of religious influence on our foreign policy, or perhaps a red herring meant to cover other political motivation.

However, it was reported that, prior to running, George Bush had no interest in the U.S. Presidency. He was quite content living as a private citizen, running his professional baseball team and so on. It was only by the urging of Bush family spiritual adviser Reverend Billy Graham, "to complete a special mission", that Bush acquiesced and ran for President.

Another disconcerting aspect of the Christian eschatological perspective is that, the final days will be preceded by the reign of the Devil or the anti-Christ. Whether referred to as Satan, Lucifer, or the Devil, most religions characterize him as the "fallen angel" that has come to usurp God's authority over man. There are many scriptural references to the Devil, with some characterizing him as a physical being, while other interpretations characterize him as ideological. In either case, he is meant to separate people from God. Many believe that Satan has been with mankind from the very beginning, with the temptation of Adam and Eve in the Garden of Eden. Much later he arrives with the temptation of Christ in the desert, where he offers him all the kingdoms of the world. Some believe that Satan's power over mankind has been increasing, following the Age of Enlightenment, as the preeminence of man and the diminished role of God as anecdotal evidence of his reign. Further, they point to ongoing wars, genocide, and abortion as evidence of a culture of death and an affirmation of an

---

[25] James A. Haught (2009-07-22). "Agog over Bush's comments on Gog and Magog". Charleston West Virginia Gazette

evil presence. The growing apostasy, the acceleration of time and rapid technological development are also considered signs that the end is approaching. However it is the secret, deceptive nature of the New World Order architects that is perhaps the most revealing and disturbing sign. For such widespread control by deception can only be accomplished by supernatural force. Like the Christ, the Anti-Christ may not be revealed to the people until the hour has come.

The Catholic Church strongly opposes any prognostication of the end times. They cite scriptural references that state "only the Father knows" when the end times will come. Nevertheless, there is plenty to suggest that the present day global political developments raise some concern within the Church.

For example, in his book, *Jesus of Nazareth*, Pope Benedict XVI refers to the evil one as the "strong man, who holds man captive (and anonymously manipulates us)." He also suggests that the tempter "does not suggest to us directly that we should worship the devil. He merely suggests we "give priority to a planned and thoroughly organized world, where God may have his place as a private concern but must not interfere with our essential purposes." He goes on to point out that the Christian is threatened today by this "anonymous atmosphere that threatens to make the faith seem ludicrous and absurd to him." But in the Christian struggle, he differentiates the enemies as more than just a particular person or persons, or even flesh and blood, but rather principalities, darkness from a host of opponents that keep coming. In reference to the apocalypse and Second Coming, he reaffirms the prophetic words in Daniel that the secular powers will rise up as four beasts based on violence and "beastial" power.[26]

While these warnings are somewhat veiled, there are other Catholic theologians who are very direct in addressing the secret societies and plans for the New World Order. Beginning in 1973, a movement within the global Catholic priesthood was initiated by a Father Stefano Gobbi in Italy. The movement was based on "interior locutions" that Fr. Gobbi was supposedly receiving from the Blessed Mother that became popular study with priests throughout the world.

The locutions centered on the crisis of faith within the Catholic Church and the world wide growing apostasy. His work studies the new atheism in a materialistic society, the view of sin as no longer immoral and the role of the media in promotion of immorality. Furthermore, he addresses a great uneasiness in the world and in the

---

[26] Jesus of Nazareth Pope Benedict the XVI.

Church that the signs of the end are emerging, but follows with the triumph of the Second Coming.

In his work, the enemies of the Church are described in several ways. One is the "Huge Red Dragon", which represents atheistic communism. The other is the "Beast Like a Leopard", which is the black beast of Freemasonry. This beast hides in the shadows and works by cunning and propaganda. This beast is described as having ten horns and ten crowns, as signs of dominion and royalty. While the goal of atheistic communism is to deny God, the aim of Freemasonry is to blaspheme Him. It promotes vices against virtues, such as pride, lust, avarice, anger, sloth, envy and gluttony thus precipitating souls into the dark slavery of evil. Then there is the "Beast like a Lamb", which is the infiltration of Masonry into the Church. This is the attempt of Satan to enter and even climb to the summit of the church, to destroy Christ and the Church and build a new idol and false church. Thus, the Antichrist will lead many souls to perdition.[27]

While the time period predicted in some of these locutions has already come to pass, it is not clear when the end or Second Coming will arrive, as this is only known by God.

Islamic eschatology is similar to Christian eschatology in that, at the appointed time, Allah will send Jesus to return to Earth to battle the Dajjal (or Devil) ushering in the new era of Messianic peace. Like Christianity, the Dajjal, is the Antichrist, who will reign prior to this time. Views on salvation based on final judgment and resurrection are fairly similar. While there are key differences in theological views, there are also many similarities.

Despite the commonalities in Christian and Islamic eschatological views, there is a history of religious conflict between Christians and Muslims. On the other hand, like most other historical conflicts, ideological differences probably played less of a role than economic issues. Likewise, present day conflicts are created by misconceptions, deliberate distortions and manipulation. It is only through deceptive influence that the current conflicts exist.

Much less known in Western culture are the multitude of Eastern religious and philosophical views on human development and rule. Confucian ideology and Taoism stress many of the same concepts of virtue, good and evil, darkness and light, truth and deception, etc. Unlike the Abrahamic religions they do not address the eschatology in the same manner, but tend to be more cosmology based. As such, they

---

[27] To The Priests, Our Lady's Beloved Sons.

focus on a person's state of being based on birth and rebirth according to how they conducted their lives.

There are some mysterious beliefs that are often attributed to secret societies. Whether these are classified as religion, philosophy, or irreligion, is really a matter of semantics. As already discussed, there are Satanic or occult connections within some secret societies. But we really don't know much about the true nature of the global elitist beliefs, as they are generally shrouded in mystery. However, we do get a glimpse of their contrarian nature relative to traditional Western and Eastern ideologies. Perhaps the motives of deceit and manipulation are purely Machiavellian in nature. However, many believe that the global elitists possess arcane knowledge from the ancient past that gives them the ability to control and manipulate humanity. Pop culture has provided some impetus to the beliefs that ancient scrolls, missing Gospels, and other physical relics possessing great powers are held within secret cabals. Supposedly, groups such as the inner circle Freemasonry possess hidden secrets connecting humanity to the divine. While this may sound far fetched, it is known that Hitler, for example, went to great lengths to try and obtain the Holy Lance that pierced the side of Christ on the cross, believing it would make him invincible.

Other occult like faiths, such as Mysticism, Gnosticism, and Kabbalism, are among the more arcane beliefs connected to secret societies and their pursuit of the divine mysteries. Some believe that today's philosopher kings have achieved mastery of these divine mysteries and have thus derived superior intellect as a result. Others believe that those who have obtained supremacy in this life have done so as a result of spiritual evolution through conduct in successive lives.

In addition to the wide variety of religious views, there are non-religious or strictly scientific views that are connected to apocalyptic predictions. In a pseudo-Freudian view of society, the apocalypse may provide the source of collective guilt for cultural super ego to finally dislodge the greatest obstacle to civilization, our tendency toward aggression against one another. This extreme event would bring the culmination in cultural evolution enabling us to love one another.

Existentialists bring a totally different outlook on the metaphysical. For example, some equate God with existence and our human struggle is embodiment of the principles of good and evil, truth and deceit, etc. By this view, individual human life is not really important, but rather, primacy is on principles. Certainly, one could go on endlessly discussing all the different philosophies but before leaving the topic, there is one other worth mentioning.

There are those that believe humans are created from aliens and much of scripture is really based on allegorical interpretations of this creation. In Jim Marrs' book Rule by Secrecy, he elaborately describes the origins of humanity based on transplanted DNA from a superior alien race, the Annunaki, into animals that inhabited the earth 500,000 years ago. He goes on to connect scriptural meaning, secret societies and wonders such as the building of The Great Pyramids to this alien heritage.[28]   Along these allegorical lines, there are inferences that "eternal fires of hell" refer to nuclear holocausts, "ascension into heaven" refers to being lifted by a type of aircraft, to a planet that gives "eternal life", where one year is equivalent to about 1000 earth years. Maars suggests that it is through the secret connection with our alien past, that the elitist powers of today derive their ability to rule.

Perhaps we are not alone in trying to sort out truth from fiction. While many speculate about the secret knowledge of the elitists, with all of their wealth, power, and influence, they may not really possess any esoteric knowledge at all. Perhaps presidents and heads of state really don't know much more than we do. They too, may be manipulated along with the rest of us, or even more so given the potential for delusion created by power. But whether it is Christian eschatology, secret scrolls or the mystery of the pyramids, the Middle East holds the keys to unlocking the secret knowledge of the ancients. Perhaps the ancient lands of Sumer and Mesopotamia still hold the keys to unlock this esoteric knowledge. Maybe there is more for U.S. troops to find in the caves of Afghanistan than the enemy.

Whatever the case, we should remain awake, for we do not know when the hour will come.

---

[28] Jim Maars. Rule by Secrecy.

Chapter 15 – What Lies Ahead?

Considering the difficulty in establishing factual history or even the present for that matter, predicting the future becomes an even greater challenge. However, the continued manipulation by those in power from behind the scenes, creating solutions to problems of their making will assuredly continue. Likewise, the agenda for the New World Order will progress.

As I talk to more people, I realize there is a growing sense of uneasiness about the direction of our nation and the world. While there will always be the oblivious, many perceive a pending crisis. Perhaps the media has fueled the uneasiness and growing discontent, with disconcerting news on economic uncertainty from mounting debt, bailouts, and unemployment. But economic concerns are only part of what seems to be ailing us. Concern over ongoing wars, terrorism, new deadly viruses, and climate change are having a destructive impact on our collective psyche. It is difficult to assess how much of this is real, and how much is intentional hype. Is the world really in trouble due to population explosion, insufficient resources, pollution, and global warming, or is it simply more control by fear?

As discussed in the last chapter, apocalyptic predictions are becoming more prevalent, especially given the Mayan prophecies associated with 2012. For those less familiar with the apocalypse, it will be characterized by the "four horsemen" which are pestilence, war, famine and death. But with all our wealth and know how, could this really happen?

One can foresee a scenario unfolding where economic collapse of the U.S. and other Western economies trigger a global depression, or perhaps further terrorist activities could be the trigger. For example, a default on foreign debt will put us at serious odds with our (primarily Asian) debt holders. Festering issues over trade, loss of jobs to Asia, and unfair competition will cause the West to blame the East. This tension has been increasing as people work harder and longer hours to try and maintain what they have, but are losing ground as they fight to compete. Perhaps China will attempt to nationalize foreign owned companies in reparation for unpaid debt. Destruction of the U.S. Dollar will result in hyperinflation and food and energy shortages will follow. Civil unrest would add fuel to the fire. Increased terrorist activities and subsequent regional conflicts would further strain the situation, with governments needing to raise money for military purposes while banks tighten the money supply. Disruption in energy supplies would add to the misery, ever increasing the chances for World War III. The potential for severe economic problems here in the U.S., a charismatic new leader who some see as a messianic figure, youth brigades, militarized police, have interesting parallels with Nazi Germany.

Technology and scientific breakthroughs that for so many years have been considered the key to setting us free and improving our lives may now be the bane of our society. When one considers the changes that have taken place over the last century, it becomes almost mind boggling. Some 1908 U.S. statistics that bear this out...

The average life expectancy was 47 years

There were 8000 cars on the road and only 144 miles of paved roads

Only 6% of Americans graduated from High School

The average wage was 22 cents/hour

Compared with the information age of today, where images and ideas can be transmitted almost instantaneously around the globe, where hand held computing power exceeds the super computers of just a couple decades earlier, where the human genome has been decoded, where more people throughout the world are foregoing personal privacy to connect through social networking sites and almost everyone can be tracked through cell phone GPS, one should occasionally pause to see if we have perhaps become so swept up in our own creation, that we begin to lose touch with our own humanity. We lose site of basics, such as the threat to our liberties by over zealous government officials. Unconfirmed rumors from a source at Sprint claim that the government requested access to 8 million cell phone records in 2008. We can no longer separate ourselves from this technology.

While there are unquestionable benefits to the appropriate use of technology in health care, business and entertainment, some of the potential pitfalls are less obvious. The Human Genome Project, which mapped the 3.1B bits of DNA information comprising the roughly 25,000 human genes, was largely funded by the U.S. Department of

Energy and National Institute of Health. The effort became international with the addition of geneticists from a number of other countries, such as the U.K., Canada and New Zealand. Ethical concerns have been raised about the motivation of the project, largely driven by the joint Clinton and Blair administrations, due to possible misuses of genetic studies on various indigenous people. The concern is that the same information that can be used to identify and target cures for diseases such as cancer and Alzheimer's, could also be used to develop bio-weapons to target people with a certain genetic make up.

Given that there is only about a 1.2% difference between the human and chimp genome, accounting for our ability to derive language, art, and philosophy, some believe understanding this part of the genome brings us closer to unlocking some esoteric design that can make humans more like the divine. Some scriptural interpretations suggest that human DNA was at one time combined with the DNA from "the sons of God", who once inhabited the earth before the time of Noah, and took human wives. They believe that the motivation for understanding and controlling this area of DNA is to enable themselves to become more Godlike. In another unusual report, there are claims that alterations of human DNA are now taking place in experiments that combine human and animal DNA, to create creatures known as Chimera. These creatures are connected to the apocalyptic ones described in Revelations. Other apocalyptic predictions based on the era of post-humanism or trans-humanism includes new forms of killer locusts, numerous diseases, and plagues.

Unquestionably, there is technology available for the manufacture of deadly viruses and diseases. Many reports have been published suggesting that AIDS was a manufactured disease and Africa its initial testing ground. Fears of mutating Swine (H1N1) or Avian (H5N1) flu viruses resulting in dangerous pandemics seem increasingly possible if not probable. In a Tom Clancy novel called *Bio Strike*, the deadly virus was actually planted in virus vaccines. Considering the similarities between the terrorist attacks of 9/11 with the plot in Clancy's *Debt of Honor* novel, maybe public fear of new vaccines is somewhat understandable.

While famine in this country seems a very remote possibility, blights on major food crops are always possible. Genetically modified crops designed to be resistant to various man made agricultural chemicals may eventually prove more susceptible to certain natural (or unnatural) blights. According to a James Martin Center for Nonproliferation Studies, the use of agro-terroristic manufactured blights have been researched by several countries, including the U.S., Canada, France, and the Soviet Union. The center listed 17 different agents that have been investigated for this purpose.

In addition to possible biological attacks on our food supply, there are concerns about the potential for intentional government intervention to exacerbate agricultural problems through control over farming resources. Due to the way agricultural subsidies work, the federal government dictates which crops, and how much are planted for the vast majority of the agriculture output in this country.

Considering the potential implications that technological developments, particularly in the biotechnology area have on our entire population, there is growing alarm over the large number of suspicious deaths of prominent scientists around the world. Scientists engaged in a wide variety of activities, many in the control of infectious diseases, have been meeting with untimely and often violent deaths. One website has actually tracked these, with 93 prominent scientists having met untimely deaths over the past decade or so.[29]

Consternation over the rapidly developing crises of economies throughout much of the world, spreading Mideast conflicts, and diseases have fueled an increasing fear that we may be heading toward the final days, the Apocalypse. While you won't see it as a lead story on the evening news or headlines in the New York Times, there is growing traffic on the Internet, late night A.M. radio, books, and other non-conventional sources that suggest we are approaching this cataclysmic event. Even pop culture is contributing to awakening apocalyptic possibilities with books and movies such as "2012".

Perhaps all this hype will lead us to the greatest, most abominable fraud ever perpetrated on mankind. In a very bizarre article published on the *Watcher Files* (www.thewatcherfiles.com) called Project Blue Beam, there is a description of an incredible NASA project the uses various technologies, implemented via satellites that will be the final component of global control. It describes what may have been contained in the secret satellite payloads that have been launched over the past several decades. According to the article, this "Blue Beam" technology can produce giant space shows; three dimensional holographic images that can be projected on to the sodium layer of the atmosphere. Messianic figures, each appropriately constructed for the target audience, accompanied by pulse microwave audio (in the appropriate language) will be projected for the audience.

---

[29] /www.stevequayle.com/index1.html

According to the article, some UFO's sightings have been attributed to the testing of the technology. Further, a documentary on the History Channel (Fall 2010) described an event whereby a lone Israeli soldier, surrounded by perhaps a hundred Lebanese troops, is aided by a legion of armed angels "that appear from the sky." The enemy troops surrender to this lone soldier, as they feared they were no match against this heavenly army.

With the world in global crisis, the plan is to create a new god, for all worlds, by using these images to dispel all prior beliefs as misinterpretations. According to the article, Project Blue Beam includes more than just audio/visual technology, but also includes the use of other types of electromagnetic radiation that can manipulate the electrical and chemical physiology of the brain. Direct "ideas" can thus be implanted in the brain or be heard as a voice from within. Apparently, the Soviets developed much in the way of this physio-psychological technology. For example, by subjecting enemies to certain types of frequencies, telepathic messaging can influence them to commit suicide. Allegedly, this type of technology has been under development by the CIA and the Defense Department to influence enemies into surrender, or to manipulate own troops into extreme feats of bravery. There have also been reports of induced heart attacks using this technology. So the same technology that can be used to encourage us kill one another, can send us a savior when we are in the most desperate need for heavenly aid.

Thus, the New World Order, the Utopian, Heaven on Earth can begin. Man and his science will reign, with control over life and death through genetic engineering and cloning or some other technology that we do not yet know about. Resources will abound for the small remaining population, all well organized into a global structure where everyone has a relatively easy role to fulfill with the aid of technology. There will no longer be concerns over war, as there are no longer any ideological differences, or individualism. The environment will revert to a condition where it was centuries ago. Benevolent kings will reign over content serfs in a New World Order that could last for the next millennium.

Conclusion

While I do not believe that the concepts in this book were supplanted into my brain via satellite transmission, I have tried to include a variety of views, including those different from my own and perhaps some that are quite far fetched. In truth, I am not so sure what constitutes far fetched, so I try to be open minded. As discussed throughout this book, people are conditioned to close mindedness, but should realize that being open minded does not need to threaten personal beliefs.

In reality, I do not think it possible for us, as serfs, to ascertain with certainty what of the previous chapters is factual, partially true, or a red herring deliberately meant to mislead us. It would be interesting to have access to the same knowledge as those who manipulate us, but then, they would lose their ability to manipulate. It would be interesting to know what, for example the President knows... Is he privy to some esoteric knowledge that is a source of power, or is he just another puppet, doing his job. When I listen to any number of past presidential speeches, I can't help but believe they are either exceptional liars, or delusional. I don't know that they are any different than any of us, in that anyone can convince themselves to the point where they actually believe something that is not the truth, or rationalize falsehoods to accept them. Perhaps intentional information firewalls are set up to give the President or key politicians "plausible deniability" on issues that would cause embarrassment if made public.

As a people, we have been trained by fear...enemies created for our own benefit. We have come to accept that our national security depends on our government keeping information from the public. By accepting this premise, we are inviting perfected global fascism. Our trust has been betrayed. The U.S. Constitution is essentially dead and powers authorized to Congress have been routinely usurped by executive orders. Once rarely used, executive orders implemented by recent administrations, number in the thousands. Under the Patriot Act, our rights as citizens have been systematically dismantled, as we can be arrested and held indefinitely without formal charge. Rumors of massive internment camps, built under the guise of being needed in the

event of massive illegal alien crackdowns, come from reliable
government sources. In reality, these prisons can be used to detain any
American citizen deemed an enemy. In truth, we no longer govern
ourselves, but are governed by the well entrenched puppet masters
operating behind the scenes. We seem to have forgotten that the
government is in place to serve the people, not the other way around.

With regard to national security, I have no doubt whatsoever,
that this nation is capable of defending itself against any outside threat,
should we actually focus on national security as a priority. However,
having U.S. troops in 130 different countries really has nothing to do
with national security. It is colonialism, plain and simple. Perhaps
some will say we need our troops to protect overseas economic
interests. If this is the case, why are there so many other nations that
are able to trade effectively in the international arena without having
troops stationed across the globe? Also, we need to consider whose
economic interests are being protected? We have exported a high
percentage of our manufacturing jobs. The average American is
working harder for a decreasing standard of living. Wealth is being
concentrated at the very top of our society, while the rest are being
lumped together in the new socialist pool.

While growing affluence throughout the world has been
attributed to the expansion of capital, we need to look at both sides of
the equation. Some figures purported extreme global poverty for 80%
of the world in 1820, down to 50% in 1950 and less than 25% by the
early 1990's. However, we need to think about where the capital came
from to effectuate this change. Was this growing affluence a result of
Adam Smith's Invisible Hand of the free markets or did it come from
another source? Would the technological advances most attributed to
the change have occurred without capitalistic influence? How much is
related to debt and who controls the debt that created the money (since
money is created out of debt)? Have we traded something very
valuable, such as our freedom or even our souls for it? Perhaps it is
something we should think about when driven by materialistic
impulses.

The control over our money and our economy by the Federal
Reserve has led us to the brink of economic disaster. With the Federal
debt now above 12 trillion, it costs Americans $1.5 billion/day in debt
service alone. This does not include unfunded social security and
Medicaid liabilities, which, according to some estimates, will add
nearly $50 trillion in the coming decades. In fact, by some estimates, it
will require 40% of the private sector output to fund social security and

Medicaid alone.[30] If one subscribes to the relationship between debt and slavery, it is easy to see that we have enslaved ourselves and all future generations as far as the eye can see. One has to wonder whether or not there will ever be repayment, or is there another part of the plan we do not know about. Undoubtedly the potential for conflict between the indebted and debt holders is very high.

Looking back over the past century, we have witnessed almost unimaginable destruction resulting from wars. People need to think very carefully about the lessons learned from the enormous human and economic costs of conflicts. Despite the glamorization of heroic military service promoted by the media, I have found that the most adamant advocates for peace are those who have had first hand experience in battle. They strongly support the notion that wars should be fought only when absolutely necessary. One needs to clearly see the distinction between the heroic soldier motivated by love of country from instigators of conflict for profit and hired mercenaries or thugs looking for the thrill of the kill.

Perhaps it is time to take another look at present day conflicts in Iraq, Afghanistan and throughout the Mideast region. The people who are being asked to sacrifice, should be asking what are we *really* doing there? Again, being led by fear and false flag operations, the true Mideast agenda remains hidden. We were told about weapons of mass destruction in Iraq, and are now engaged in Afghanistan against the same enemy we armed and trained. With possible sanctions against Iran, one has to wonder, what is our agenda there? Will we have the same success as the sanctions that were associated with the deaths of 500,000 children in Iraq, which we can then call a success? If success means galvanizing hatred against us, we will certainly succeed and we will certainly make life more dangerous for ourselves. If we are looking for Iran to capitulate, what do we want them to surrender? Should they give up their government and allow us to install one that is to our liking like our CIA did in the late 1950's? Are we asking them to give up their religious ideologies? We have heard about nuclear ambitions, which can not be for peaceful purposes, despite Iran importing about 40% of their energy needs. Unfortunately, we bear responsibility for not holding our so called representatives accountable for actions taking place in the region. We are not getting the truth and not pushing hard enough for it because we don't want to be considered unsupportive. I think Congressman Ron Paul said it most accurately,

---

[30] Ron Paul. The Revolution.

"truth is treason in the empire of lies."[31]   Perhaps the real reason for conflict has to do with religious fundamentalism…maybe there is just no place for it in the New World Order.

However, this should raise concern for people of all faiths, and even more so for people who have lost their faith, having had it stolen by the tide of secularism. The growing apostasy in Europe and North America is not necessarily by coincidence. There are those who have been deliberately attacking all faiths believing it has no place within the New World Order. Perhaps religion can be tolerated, but only to the extent that it does not interfere with global fascist control. Unfortunately, most people have become so indoctrinated by media spoon fed information, they are unable to think beyond the images and sounds on television. Anything beyond our five senses and outside our spatial-temporal recognition can't exist. The difficulty is in training our thinking to recognize deception and to stop lying to ourselves because we don't want to face a painful truth.

There is a saying that "you can only serve one master". People need to decide who that master will be. If we sink completely into earthly deprivation and materialistic pursuits, we lose what connects us to the divine. We become earthly animals, not much different than ants building their colonies. When we seek to be like the divine, we reject the empty promises of earthly possessions, striving for higher aspirations. There is much to learn from scripture, as it holds timeless knowledge to guide mankind through this life. Perhaps as many believe, it holds the absolute truths, and those truths will set us free. For people of faith, there is the belief that God has a plan for humanity. From the determinist perspective, perhaps all that has happened is to fulfill that plan as it is written. As a simple serf, I have no special knowledge of how one should conduct oneself, how we fit into God's plan, or the timing of things to come. But I know from faith that as individuals, we are called to conduct ourselves in a virtuous way, despite what goes on around us. Maybe not much has changed in two millennia, as the Greek philosopher Epictetus noted back in 55 B.C. that we can't control external forces, only our response to them.

As I have said all along, I am just a serf. I am not an exegete on epistemology, nor do I have any special knowledge or insight into the political machinations of this world. I can only judge what I see in this world based on my own frame of reference. Is it unfathomable that someone is sitting somewhere, deciding that crashing passenger jets

---

[31] Ron Paul. The Revolution.

into tall buildings is ultimately for the overall good? From my simple minded view, it appears of evil design, but who am I to say. I think most people whether of deistic beliefs or not, have an inherent sense of right and wrong, good and evil, whatever their source. We still have free will and if we can look beyond our cultural brain washing, we can exercise it in a responsible manner. Probably the most important step in this direction is to stop living in fear. People need to get beyond the media hype over crises and terror that limit the ability to think. They also need to shed the belief that blind support of government policy is patriotic...it definitely is not. Fascism is very anti-American and expression against it and support of Constitutional rights is very pro American. If we keep heading down the current New World Order global path, being American or supporting what it stands for will be meaningless. All sovereign nations will be destroyed and we will all be simple serfs of the global society. If we look to serve a higher purpose we can get beyond the apathy and nihilism that is so pervasive and have hope in our future here on earth and beyond this world.

While some may think this point ridiculous, we really need to think very seriously about what it means to be free and whether or not we want it. To help illustrate this point, there was a Warner Brothers film released in 1999 by the Wachowski brothers called *"The Matrix."* The sci-fi film was about a computer controlled society, where reality for humans was simulated by computers. The protagonists of the story were computer programmers who were able to connect and disconnect from the Matrix, with the objective of setting humans free from this computer controlled illusion. The film was an allegorical representation of modern day media controlled societies. In it, there is one who ultimately controls reality, and the masses who live their lives of illusion. The illusion is easy for people compared with the harsh realities outside the Matrix. There is a scene where one of the rebels, Cypher, betrays the others who are working against the Matrix, as he finds the unplugged reality too harsh compared with the comforts of the Matrix. This allegory seems very appropriate today where many Americans would rather live the American dream, than wake up to face the harsh realities of where we have been led as a society. The choice is ours whether we go on accepting lies, or unplug from the Matrix.

There is no doubt in my mind that we, as a society are much less free than we were a generation ago. While changes have been subtle, they are quite remarkable. As a very simple example, I look back to going into New York City as a young adult. Midtown was full of pornographic establishments. Prostitution and drug peddling were conducted in relatively plain view of all. Today, under the watchful eyes of thousands of cameras, just light up a cigarette on an outdoor platform; Even with no signs posted, you will be immediately accosted by police and treated as a criminal. This is just a very simple example of how we have gone from the abuse of freedom to a "nanny state" mentality in just a very short period of time. If we look at the lawlessness that occurred post hurricane Katrina, we see another example of why freedom can not be the same as lawlessness, and comes with a lot of individual responsibility.

People have often spurned religions as having too many rules that impose upon our personal freedoms. However, many of these, which are really about living virtuously, actually allow us to live more freely. If you look at the wisdom in many of the religious or philosophical beliefs, be it Confucian theory to live nobly and compassionately, or live by the Golden Rule, you realize that the more we control our own actions, the freer we are from control by others. When we act responsibly, charitably, and out of care for one another, we act for freedom. Recklessness, disregard for others, avarice and greed lead people to seek remedy from the government, more laws and more enforcement. Probably more than anything else, greed is ultimately responsible for the destruction of humanity and freedom.

Anytime we look to the government to solve our problems we take away from our own freedom. Self sufficiency and responsibility is obviously then key to freedom. How often have we seen government programs put in place that run counter to self sufficiency? Unless we can provide for ourselves and one another, government bureaucratic redistribution will do it for us.

Aside from personal actions, people need to be more aware of the impact of technological development on our freedom and humanity. Scientific development need not be the most important element of our human existence. It must come with appropriately balanced ethical guidelines that respect humanity and natural law. People need to think through possible problems created in providing solutions for other issues.

Finally, ignorance is probably the greatest deterrent of all to our freedom. Our educational process should continue throughout our lives and include a real understanding of ourselves and the world around us, including as Plato put it, issues of the State. Formal education should be well rounded, providing language, literature and philosophy that inspire creativity, factual history that facilitates appreciation of freedom and liberty, as well as math and science that can be applied to meeting human needs.

Perhaps media and educational mind control have led us away from the path of freedom and self reliance, or perhaps it is our own undoing. Whether the NWO is a foregone conclusion, or whether we can still determine our own future is not clear. Even if there is no turning back from this new global organizational structure, there is still hope for a bright future. A controlled global economy, where goods and services are concentrated in regions best suited for their production, for example, oil and energy production from the Mideast, China as the manufacturing center for non-durables, Japan for autos, Germany for chemicals, the U.S. for banking and insurance, etc., may provide a highly efficient model. Everyone will have a role and with technological developments, we may eventually be able to work less. People could be offered the highest quality sports, entertainment and plenty of other distractions. Resources, such as food and medicine will be apportioned by the government and population will be controlled according to government mandates. There will be no more wars over geographic boundaries or religion, since these will not exist as they do today. The environment will return to more pristine state, as tighter global regulation will better control pollution. Maybe we will all ride our bicycles to work, dressed in our gray flannels. As Marx so aptly described it, man can achieve his best through is work.

Despite meeting needs of the population and bringing prevailing peace, the question remains, are the societal engineers, the philosopher kings good or evil? Perhaps rule by deception should give us our first clue. Mass human destruction based on greed, attacks on religion and freedom should also factor in to our thinking. We also need to consider who and how many of us will even participate in this NWO...are those who suggest an ideal global population of 500,000,000 correct? Who and how will they judge the living and the dead? Perhaps they can justify killing 6.5 billion as "collateral damage" to bring about this utopian world. Maybe the dead would be the fortunate ones, as they would not become soulless androids.

Whatever the real truth may be, it is time for people to wake up and find it. I strongly encourage anyone reading this not to accept what I have written as truth, but seek the truth themselves...For the truth will set us Serfs free.

Afterword

When I started this project, I knew conceptually what I wanted to talk about, but did not have a good idea as to where it might all lead, how long it would take me to express these ideas, or what the end product might look like. Although this is a first for me, I feel a certain advantage over many professional authors in that I did not write with the intent to profit from it. I have a regular, full time job that takes care of my financial needs. Nor I am looking for any notoriety. This is strictly written in the interest of sharing ideas with others who might be open minded enough to explore them.

While I realize how controversial this subject matter can be, I hope you found it interesting and feel inspired to continue learning more on your own. Hopefully we can bring real change for peace and liberty, but if nothing else, strive for betterment of ourselves. For those others who feel I should probably be forced to drink hemlock, I did warn you up front.

While I initially found the revelation of such widespread conspiracy very disturbing, I now find a certain peace in knowing what I know and more importantly, understanding what I don't know. It is my hope that all of you will find this same peace and will enjoy what you have, whether a lot or a little, and not be motivated by excesses that create destruction of others. I hope you will aspire to the virtuous ideals that set humankind above all other species.

For thousands of years, man has pursued an understanding of the truth. It is a uniquely human experience and we are defined by how we conduct ourselves in this quest. No other animal pursues truth, faith, or eternal life. Perhaps life is really all about the journey.

Part Two: Demystifying Political Economy

Introduction

For those who have read my earlier polemic on global conspiracy theory entitled *Serfs and Kings, Demystifying Political Economy* will have a familiar tone. While the former was a general discourse on the philosophy and history of global domination by secret elite, the latter is intended to be a brief exegesis of how world economies have developed and how this development has been managed by the same secret elite.

Demystifying Political Economy is written from the perspective of a non-economist, and it is therefore, not my intent to write "Economics for Dummies". From the perspective of a well studied economist, this essay may rightly be considered rubbish; however, given economics as an inexact science, not subject to laws of physics and mathematics, and given such wide disagreement among the best minds in the field on how economies can best be managed, I take poetic license excusing myself from a scientific approach to the subject and move forward in exploring the political nature of the beast, unencumbered by too much knowledge of the subject.

Similar to my earlier work in "Serfs and Kings", my intent is more philosophical; to expose the reader to some alternative views on the development of economic systems and to stimulate thought about where we find ourselves today and what possibly lies ahead. For most of us find ourselves completely absorbed by the "system", an increasingly complex economic environment that has evolved from individuals and family units, to small business communities, to national economies and now globally connected economies. We probably rarely, if ever, think about how or why we got here, or, whether it is for better or worse. Unless you are part of a very elite few, it is unlikely that you understand whether the evolutionary process was based on natural law, or manipulated by unnatural forces with the resources to do so. We probably rarely consider whether or not the system is free, fair, or if can it be changed since we are powerless in it.

However, there is to some extent, an awakening to social and political change taking place around the world as more people engage in dialogue on the subject, primarily due to the fallout over global economic crises. Perhaps the delusion of being in control or the apathy in the political economic process is coming to an end. My attempt to

Demystify Political Economy will answer some questions, but will likely generate just as many. Without being behind the scenes, it is impossible to know the motivations behind national and international directives that move us one way or another. However, as we witness the political economies of nations converging into a global economy in what appears a Hegelian Capitalism Thesis + Socialism Antithesis → Synthesis manner, hopefully what is presented here will serve as food for thought about the forces, be it natural or contrived that are bringing us into this new direction. For it is very likely that our future, like our past, will be shaped by how well we understand and manage the new global economy, given the inextricable link between economics, politics, war and peace.

Chapter 1 - Economic Basics, Wealth and Poverty

As mentioned in my introduction, my intent is not to instruct on the theories of economics, however it is necessary to establish some basic understanding of some key concepts on which to build.

The first is a basic understanding of the laws of supply and demand. Supply is the quantity of inputs and outputs, i.e., "goods and services that people are ready to sell at various prices within some given period of time, other factors beside price being constant."[32] Supply can include inputs such as land, natural resources, energy, labor, capital, technology, managerial skills, as well as finished goods and services.

The flip side of supply is demand. Demand is defined by needs and wants, or the "quantity of a good or service that people are ready to buy at various prices within some given time period, other factors besides price held constant."[33] Another key concept in economics is scarcity of resources, which is simply the condition by which there are insufficient resources in production, consumption and distribution to satisfy all the needs and wants of a specified group.[34]

The relationship between these three concepts forms the basis for understanding an economic system and their relationship will be important throughout this analysis. Therefore, it is probably worth a little discussion into the role that each serves. Beginning with demand, most people understand a hierarchy of needs and wants. Certain basic physiological needs of food, shelter and the like are obvious, followed by the next tier of wants, such as security, property ownership, transportation, and finally more refined personal preferences. In terms of traditional psychological theory, esteem and self actualization, the top of the personal hierarchy, create demands that are unique to all of us. Supply is created by the combination of natural resources along with labor, management, technology, and capital. It can be centrally controlled, or controlled by producers in a free market, depending upon

---

[32] Keat, Young. Managerial Economics
[33] Ibid.
[34] Ibid.

what is being supplied and the societal structure in which it takes place. Scarcity of resources simply means that the supply of wants will always exceed societies' productive ability to satisfy all of them.

As basic as it may sound, do people really understand what wealth and poverty mean? In truth, both are relative terms and mean different things to different people. Most people think in terms of monetary or property wealth, but physical, spiritual, and emotional wealth are of equal or greater importance then monetary wealth to most. While most of this discussion is focused on the abundance or scarcity of consumable goods, it is important to bear in mind that there is a broader sense of wealth and poverty. While there is often the misperception that wealth is necessarily good while poverty bad, by this definition, there is no measure of personal well being or happiness directly connected with wealth and poverty. Generally, most believe that there is some balance between having enough, and not being consumed with, or by the pursuit of physical goods.

While we don't typically look at wealth from an economic class system perspective here in the U.S., one could categorize it as such. At the bottom is the below poverty class. This would include the indentured (although slavery is now illegal) and those without the basic needs to survive, or those that can survive only as beneficiaries of charity from others. The next class would be the impoverished, who through their toil can only meet basic needs with great difficulty. This is followed by the middle class, where most of us fall. One could also call this the working class, which can be further divided between low middle, middle, and upper middle. Following the working class is the free class. This can be viewed as the investing class, or independently wealthy, where there are enough assets to generate income to satisfy needs without labor. There can be a broad range of wealth in this class, depending upon the level of personal needs. If ones' needs are very simple, less wealth is required, while more extravagant needs and wants require a much higher asset base. Inheritance and pelf are generally thought to be the greatest source of wealth in this class. Some may opt to work in this class, but more so as a hobby. Finally we have the ruling class. This includes the top echelon of the wealthy, very powerful politicians and corporate kings, with the apex of this class being those who control central banks and the high ranking politicians. The top of this group works behind the scenes to establish global economic and foreign policies, while deciding sanctions against uncooperative nations. They are not elected officials, but self appointed "philosopher kings" who by nature of their wealth and power, can manipulate political outcomes. They are the architects of society with the primary goal of retaining the political and economic gains won throughout history.

Chapter 2 – Some History

I am always a bit reluctant about giving historical perspective, considering my skepticism on what is actual historical fact versus fabrications, or other deliberate and non-deliberate misleading information. However, I will make some assumptions taking certain premises as true for a basis from which to start.

With regard to political economies, historians believe formal economic structures have been in place for thousands of years. An early form of capitalism, called "chrematistics" has been around for several millennia. We know about this form from writings of Aristotle, who was vocal in his opposition of chrematistics, which is the accumulation of wealth from selling items above their appropriate value, i.e., for profit. The key difference between modern capitalism and chrematistics is that chrematistic economy is based on "use value" of the goods produced and "exchange value" relative to required inputs, i.e., they will produce profit once the values of the inputs are deducted. Capitalism is similar in terms of profit motive, but based on "market value" derived from supply and demand. Despite opposition to making profit, Aristotle promoted the idea that the circulation of money was the source of boundless riches, not unlike the consumerism philosophy of today.

Capitalism, which is an economic system based on private ownership, has existed in various forms throughout much of our known history. For example, in the Middle Ages, control and the "accumulation of capital" was connected with mercantilism, a close relative of capitalism. Characteristics of the early capitalistic and mercantile systems, such as national hoarding of gold and silver as ersatz currency, gave way to laissez faire capitalism as described by early economists, such as Adam Smith. With regard to modern day economic theory, Adam Smith's *The Wealth of Nations* published in 1776 is probably the most renowned work of its kind, as it was the benchmark for promoting free economies for centuries. Regular reference will be made to this work for Smith's poignant insights into the nature of capitalistic society.

In viewing political economy and the factors influencing wealth and poverty, one needs to consider both the individual and collective factors, of a nation or as nations. Going back just a couple hundred years, agriculture was at the primary basis of wealth. For without food, farming and husbandry, there is only the struggle for survival. So prior to the Industrial Revolution, the view of societies was primarily agrarian, where people produced to accommodate their own needs, or those within a family or feudal system. The feudal system provided some protection for the serfs, in that it offered joint defense against outside threats. There was very limited production of goods in excess of basic necessities for the non-property owning peasants and their feudal masters; therefore, there was very limited trade.

As agricultural capabilities developed, particularly with the advent of machinery to replace man and beast, production in excess of that which was needed for personal consumption could be achieved. These excesses could be exchanged for other goods, thus allowing for the expansion into merchant markets and trade. The post-feudal world saw the development of towns, which employed craftsman and mechanics who exchanged their wares primarily with the country farmers. For the most part, exchanges were based on attaining enough for very basic subsistence.   Along with the associated excess agricultural production, towns and crafts flourished and with a variety of goods being produced in excess of local needs, trade increased. With basic needs increasingly met, excesses could then be used in the trade or purchase of convenience or luxury items. Often these items were brought from far away lands, and were purchased using gold or silver money, which could be transported more easily over distances compared with physical goods.

In addition to agricultural development, new knowledge to uncover and utilize natural resources, land, energy, minerals, etc., was becoming available, as were better developed shipping lanes for the movement of consumable goods.   With these developments that facilitated the system of excess production and sale came an increasing generation of profit. Profit, which can be defined several ways, as accounting, economic, etc., in general, refers to the amount of revenue or exchange value above cost of inputs. Along with profits, capital to invest and build without only relying solely on operating profits to finance projects contributed to the increased rate of enterprise growth over the past centuries.

Further supporting the development of towns and the decline of the feudal system was the establishment of stronger governments, under whose protection and regulation trade could be reasonably exist. It was the ideological shift attributed to the Age of Enlightenment, bestowing basic human rights on mankind which was critical in enabling this new form of economic development by granting certain protections under law. The abolition of slavery was a natural evolution of enlightenment; that man was to produce for himself of free will, not for a ruler under threat or punishment. In addition, the pursuit of wealth, once considered evil by many of the religious, was no longer viewed in this regard. In the classic sense of enlightenment, government's role was limited to defense of liberty, where man was under the rule of law rather than the rule of men. However, as will be discussed in more detail, not everyone believes that true freedom exists today and that people now work harder than slaves, who were motivated only by survival.

Early in the commercial development process, there was a natural order for the application of capital based on ease of getting a return. Unlike today, where tremendous flows of capital go into foreign markets based on perceived risk and rewards, the idea during this early industrial era was to invest locally as a first choice, and look at investing in foreign trade only if no opportunities lent themselves locally. Solid foundations of international economic systems were taking hold by the mid 18th century.

However, what really contributed to unprecedented economic growth was The Industrial Revolution. Most consider the period beginning in the 18th and into the 19th century, as the onset of this technological revolution. The advent of mechanized textile manufacturing, followed by steam powered engines, iron founding, etc., spread from Britain, across Europe and into North America. These innovations had a profound effect on society. The topic is worthy of volumes by itself in terms of the socioeconomic changes brought about by centralized industrial production and manufacturing centers. Clearly, there was a change in wealth creation and distribution, shifting much away from the traditional ruling class power to the new industrialists. There was incredible wealth creation, as new industries provided greatly expanded commerce, lifting so many from poverty. According to statistics, 80% of the world lived in "extreme poverty" in 1820, declining to less than 25% by 1990, driven by technological change. On the other hand, this change also brought about a new breed of greedy and abusive masters.

As commerce based on new manufacturing capabilities and trade continued to expand, the organization of those activities into a "political economy" was perhaps a natural course of events. One needs to consider some history to gain perspective on how this organization took place and continues to evolve. But before leaving this topic, it is worth noting that the level of technological development has been so incredible over such a short span, that there are those who believe that "enlightenment", both in terms of technology and the humanistic self determination by rule of law, was more than just evolutionary. Some attribute "extraordinary" outside influences as being responsible for the enlightenment of man leading to the rapid development that will follow. Perhaps there is a mysterious link between the new found enlightenment and the conflicts and trade offs that follow.

Chapter 3 - Development of Political Economy

In exploring economic systems, one can start with the most basic, i.e., the individual, and work to the increasingly complex, from familial, feudal, community, state, national, regional (multi-national), and finally global system. Supply and demand dynamics exist within each structure and increase in complexity as this environ grows.

For purposes of this discussion I will use the Industrial Revolution as the starting point from which to trace the evolution of current global system in which we now find ourselves.

As previously mentioned, the 1800's ushered in the development of new machinery and electric power to replace what was previously accomplished through man or beast. Factories replaced home or cottage industries and more and more workers left their farms for employment in these factories. This Revolution spread through much of Europe between 1820 and 1850, followed by the U.S. from about 1860 on.

Out of this Revolution came tremendous social and political change, as great fortunes for the captains of industry grew, giving them new found political power where it had been tightly held by ruling aristocracy for so many years prior. In what became a good marriage, the industrialists and governing rulers created a formidable force for expansion of economic and political power. In what tends to get distorted or glossed over in our elementary history studies was this period of capitalistic imperialism. Armies became the means by which imperialistic nations secured resources, such as raw materials and trading partners for the empires that were being constructed by the captains of industry and the governments they controlled. Colonies were established in foreign territories, giving claim or "national interest" to the nation from which the colony came. For example, by 1875, British territories included India, Canada, Australia, as well as numerous smaller territories across the globe, used as commercial centers. Other nations, including Germany, France, Italy, Japan, and the U.S. were expanding as well. By establishing colonies in foreign lands, military action could be justified when such action suited political purposes. Often, governments including the U.S., would use idealism to justify sending armies abroad to "spread democracy" to these other lands. What was called "Manifest Destiny" in the U.S. had similar counterparts in other nations, such as Germany.

Advantageous treaties of commerce with colonies provided monopoly outlets for the merchants of the countries who established them. Hostilities over trade were commonplace. As an early example England prohibited delivery of goods by shippers other than their own, citing it as a national security issue. Their rationale was that it was necessary to keep British ships and naval personnel employed. This inflamed the Dutch who were preeminent European shippers resulting in conflict between the two nations. Likewise, tariffs were also a reason to war as evidenced by the war between the French and Dutch in 1672 over retaliatory tariffs. Aside from these local conflicts, the "colonialism" or "imperialism", that would continue to grow across Africa, Asia, and the Pacific Islands, fomented tensions among the global powers that would eventually leading to WWI.

In addition to international trade tensions, domestic tensions arose within the workplace, as factory workers were forced to work long hours and endure what were often sub-human conditions. A major change for the working class emerging out of the Industrial Revolution was the division of labor. This simply means that a process to produce goods was broken down into specific tasks in order to produce most efficiently.

The role of labor in society has been discussed for thousands of years, with references to division of labor in Plato's Republic; where the minimum state is considered to require a farmer, a builder, a weaver, a shoemaker and perhaps one or two others to meet the basic bodily needs of the people. The labor topic becomes central to theorists that follow, such as Adam Smith and later Karl Marx, in that out of this division of labor, evolves highly refined skills to greatly increase productivity, but also the "mental mutilation" of the individual and the "alienation of self". So within the same division of labor, we have the matching of skills, potentially the stimulus for technological advancement by those who are focused on a task, but the destruction of ones own freedom to grow and pursue true desires or labors of love.

Historical perspective may be in the eye of the beholder. While some would claim a victory by the expansion of democratic ideals through trade, the wealth and power created by this new industrial might, sponsored by governments and their armies, became more concentrated into elitist factions. In the meantime, worker dissatisfaction continued to grow, as workers faced inhumane conditions at the hands of their capitalist masters. Although not really a new phenomenon, as earlier theorists such as Smith pointed out:

"We rarely hear, it has been said, of the combinations of masters, though frequently of those of workmen. But whoever imagines, upon this account, that masters rarely combine, is as ignorant of the world as of the subject. Masters are always and everywhere in a sort of tacit, but constant and uniform, combination, not to raise the wages of labour above their actual rate...Masters, too, sometimes enter into particular combinations to sink the wages of labour even below this rate. These are always conducted with the utmost silence and secrecy till the moment of execution; and when the workmen yield, as they sometimes do without resistance, though severely felt by them, they are never heard of by other people" In contrast, when workers combine, "the masters...never cease to call aloud for the assistance of the civil magistrate, and the rigorous execution of those laws which have been enacted with so much severity against the combination of servants, labourers, and journeymen."[5]

Inspired by abusive capitalistic imperialism and harsh labor practices, came new schools of philosophical thought, including such notable writings of socialist ideals by Germany's Karl Marx. The new socialistic or populist agenda put forth by Marx and others became a growing threat to the ruling elite. While force was generally used against worker and labor movements, a more effective means of control was needed. As inspired by Hegelian thinking, the appropriate synthesis would eventually take root by controlling both the capitalistic thesis and the socialist antithesis. In countries such as Russia, where the burgeoning democratic socialist revolution was taking hold, British and U.S. interests took control by backing a new group of socialists, the Bolsheviks.

Even Marx himself became strongly influenced by agents of Lord Palmerton's British foreign office. Under the guidance of the likes of Palmerton, U.S. and British banking agents Cecil Rhodes, Jacob Schiff, Lord Milner and with support from President Wilson (and later Roosevelt), Trotsky and his followers subverted the potential success of a democratic revolution that would have otherwise taken place. Using agencies such as the Red Cross as a cover to support Bolshevik instigators and recruit former Russian POW's (from war against Japan) to become seeds in the Revolution, the populist movement was defeated from within. Thus developed a state that was completely different from the ideological state; one free from government and without need of an army. Because of Russia's support against Germany, all this must be kept secret, especially from the British citizens who would not understand the deliberate destruction of an important ally.[35]

Some speculate that elitist dislike for the anti-Semitic Russian Czar was the motivation for Bolshevik support. Others speculate on the prospect for financial gain by backing a regime that would give them access to mining and other important industries. Most likely, it was the "support both sides of the conflict" formula at work, which was used so successfully by the powerful European financiers in most of the conflicts throughout modern history. This enables one to hedge ones bet until the outcome becomes clear.

Whatever the case, general anti-religious sentiment was a key component of Marxist philosophy. According to Marx and his supporters, religion was the "opiate of the masses", holding people down from achieving true freedom and human progress. Perhaps fueled by the historical abuse by powerful clergy, religious destruction was perhaps at the strategic core of Communist promotion. However, this premise would fuel the ideological divide that would set up a century of global conflict, be it outright war or of the Cold War variety.

So people are left to choose between two evils...on the one hand, we have the freedoms associated with our democratic capitalistic society, including the freedom to compete against one another and be used and manipulated by the capitalistic machine versus the State controlled society where everyone is a "Comrade" but there is no religious freedom.

So has the fear of Communism been engrained in our thinking, we have fought numerous wars, sacrificed countless lives and built arsenals that could destroy the population of the world several times over without most of us really understanding what the movement meant. Even a discussion about the topic is considered un-American to many, while at the same time we accept that our own government operates in increasing secrecy, waging secret wars using our CIA and coordinated clandestine operations with other governments around the world. We accept that Presidential powers have grown excessively, far surpassing those granted by The Constitution, particularly when it comes to waging wars.

---

[35] Griffin, G. Edward, Creature from Jekyll Island.

While there were two Red Scares in the U.S., thanks to laws enacted to protect us from ourselves, Communism appears to be no longer a threat. Also, culturally, we have been dumbed down enough so that even a discussion of any "Communist like" ideal is taboo. This reflects a pure anti-intellectualism culture. Despite such strong opposition to Communism, it is interesting to note that following WWII, the U.S. continued to fund Russian industrial development, including military development, all funded by loans backed by U.S. taxpayers. These loans funded weaponry that the Soviets would supply our enemies for later use against U.S. troops.

What is also puzzling is that Communism formed in Revolution and violence simply went quietly into the night to become social democracy, just as the converse is true here in the U.S. Once the Russian socialistic system failed to produce enough to feed itself and had to go to borrow from the IMF to buy grain, Communist submission was inevitable.

Aside from support of Communist Russia, funds from the U.S. and the World Bank freely flowed into a wide variety of industries in China, despite claims of human rights violations. China joined the World Bank in 1980, giving it access to billions in low to no interest loans. Western loans of $10B virtually disappeared in support of new social democracies, but the unpaid loans were secured by the taxpayers of the lending countries. Such behind the scenes transfer of wealth from richer to poorer nations is common, with the justification being to "keep a country from becoming Communist, or from falling under terrorist control." In reality, money buys influence, loyalty and privilege in the countries from the tyrants who run them.

We don't know for certain the realities of the Cold War. The massive military build ups, the race for space, certainly created unprecedented military might. Perhaps that was the point of it all. Why would we otherwise support such use of taxpayer funds for such massive nuclear arsenals? Perhaps it is conflict for the sake of conflict, or just another means of controlling the masses by controlling both sides of the conflict.

However cleverly crafted to produce the framework by which our social structures are formed, it is worthy to draw some comparisons between the two systems. As we look at the ideologies, we should also remember the lives lost in defense of both sides of the conflict.

Chapter 4 - Wars and Trade

Perhaps British Statesman Cecil Rhodes, founder of DeBeers (and Rhodesia, now called Zimbabwe), summed up the preceding centuries best in his quote proclaimed while viewing the vastness of the out of reach stars, "If I could, I would annex other planets".[36]
Wars over control of economies and trade have been going on since the beginning of recorded history. Again, I preface discussions of history as being nationalistically biased, and generally in the eyes of the victor. I can only rely on what I have learned from a variety of written sources and discussion with limited personal acquaintances from other nations. While most of us have learned about the ideological bases for wars, especially those involving our own nation, we tend not to probe deeply enough to uncover the true causes of most wars, which are generally economic. With regard to wars over trade, the Europeans certainly had the lead on the U.S., as their colonization efforts began before we were a nation and were strengthened prior to the establishment of the U.S. as a military power. Spanish and British conquests built extensive empires for expanding trade and resource bases before the U.S. gained its independence. France, Russia, Germany, Holland, Italy also expanded their trade influences during the 18th and 19th centuries. Trade alliances were often formed to pressure nations to adopt very one-sided trade treaties. For example, a few years after Admiral Perry pushed into Japan, the nation was forced to sign a very favorable trade treaty to the benefit of the U.S., Britain, Holland, Russia and France. The humiliation created by this treaty fueled Japan's resolve to become a strong military power, which would play prominently on the World War stage. Even among supposed allies, competition for the spoils of victory would pit one side against the other.

Our own nation has not been immune from economic aspirations, even from the onset. While the Declaration of Independence cited a long list of tyrannies against the British crown, there is substantial evidence to suggest that many of the influential American statesmen were also motivated by financial reasons to pursue

---

[36] ^ S. Gertrude Millin, *Rhodes*, London, 1933, p.138

independence. British restrictions over our trade, imposition of taxes, duties, and British banking over sight had a very limiting effect on the economic potential of the American colonists, particularly those with significant business interests. It was common during the period for colonies to be under the economic control of the country from whence they came. From the British perspective, they viewed themselves (and the French) as the most liberal in terms of trade treaties with their colonies, particularly compared with Spain and Portugal. In addition to providing a market for colonial goods, they also supplied military protection to their colonies, which allowed them unfettered passage overseas.

Evidence suggests that even the American Civil War was fought more so over economic issues than slavery. European interests were backing the South against the North in return for favorable trade treatment on cotton raw materials for textiles. Lincoln played the "slave card" only after realizing that European interests might support the South, and thus swayed public opinion to counter this move.[37]

Most of the U.S. colonization efforts were based in the Americas. Manifest Destiny, which had similar doctrinal counterparts in other countries, gave us the resolve as "the ordained people of God" to expand westward against Mexico. As an example, following the Napoleonic Wars, Russia, Prussia, and Austria formed what was called the Holy Alliance to promote Christian values of charity and peace in European life, although the contrarian view suggests it was designed to maintain the monarchies in the face of possible revolution. The Monroe Doctrine, signed in 1823 basically stated that any actions by Europeans to colonize in the Americas would be viewed as an act of aggression that would be responded to by U.S. intervention. In return, the U.S. would also agree not to interfere with European colonies. South Americans viewed this doctrine as basically laying claim to South America as a U.S. possession. The British and Russians supported the U.S. with their military, in exchange for allowing trade access, which would not have been possible under control of Spain. In later years, the Monroe doctrine was expanded by the Roosevelt Corollary, which basically gave the U.S. the right to intervene against any perceived European influence in the Americas.

At the same time, tensions over Spain's rule in Western territories were fed by the Newspapers sensationalism, i.e., "yellow journalism". They portrayed a cruel authority over Cuba opposing the

---

[37] Griffin, G. Edward. The Creature from Jekyll Island.

Cuban people's efforts to gain independence. The U.S. sent the battleship Maine to Havana harbor to protect U.S. citizens there, when a "mysterious" explosion sunk the ship. The event was used as the flashpoint to declare war against Spain. The U.S. victory gained the important port island territories of Puerto Rico, Guam, Cuba and the Philippines.

As colonial powers staked out claims across the globe, forming trading partners, alliances and treaties, hostilities grew between the competing alliances over the economic benefits. This of course, becomes the underlying basis for the two World Wars that leave some 80 million dead. Economics and power go hand in hand, and the Great Wars of the 20th century galvanized political and economic power for the U.S. and its Allies. With this power also came the ability to impose ideology on the defeated, which some consider the greatest of all human egotistical wants. Thus was the end result of WWII.

As it has also been said, "nothing can be won from beggars", the first goal of the post war victors was to rebuild broken nations. Anarchy and revolution were obviously enemies to those in power and whether by social conditioning or oppression, needed to be eliminated. After WWII, the Marshall Plan pumped $13B (which was at one time a lot of money) on top of nearly the same amount provided during the war, in economic and technological aid to rebuild Europe. Aid was also offered to the Soviet Union, but was not accepted. Aside from its purpose to rebuild industrial engines, break down trade barriers, and build infrastructure, the aid also served to help integrate Europe and prevent the spread of Communism, especially to France and Italy, which were considered vulnerable. As some might speculate, there were strings attached. The U.S. insisted on access to make economic assessments of any country accepting aid, and political pressure could then be applied to make certain trade agreements. The Soviets saw the plan as a Wall Street contrived imperialistic device to enslave Europe. They offered the Molotov Plan as an alternative, designed to provide aid in the form of trade subsidies, but could not match the value of the U.S. plan. Most of the aid was targeted toward the purchase of U.S. goods, but foreign governments could also use the funds to create new loans, government spending projects, or shore up their currency. The majority of Marshall Plan money, except that loaned to Germany, was never repaid. Japan also did not receive Marshall Plan money, but benefitted substantially from the U.S. and United Nations Korean War spending. The success of the Marshal Plan is still debated. Some consider it very successful, while others believe it interfered with free market development (which proved very successful in Japan), and was simply used to corrupt.   GATT agreements were also one of the outcomes in the wake of WWII, with subsequent agreements to follow.

While some will argue the ideological merits of the wars over the past couple centuries and probably those of the past millennium, the truth is quite unavoidable…wars are fought for those with economic stakes and are supported by media influence and the governments they support. The rest of the people involved are just pawns. Some might also argue that the economic importance of conflicts is secondary to the ideological outcomes but with wealth and power comes the ability to implement and control ideology. Our lives are temporal, but ideas are not.   If control over ideology can only occur from a position of economic strength, then one could say "the ends justify the means." Taken to an extreme, an Opium War in Afghanistan that provides economic resources to fight secret ideological wars justifies the collateral damage of countless American and Russian heroine addicts. It also implies that money and materialism ultimately determine our conduct.

Currently, the U.S. sits at the summit of power, although maybe not for much longer. Perhaps throughout the world, everyone is looking for our demise; maybe even our allies secretly plot against us. Maybe our alliances, overt and covert are loyal…we really don't know what goes on behind the scenes in the power struggle for global domination. Hence, the current economic crisis could very well have been designed by other foreign powers, just as some speculate that American and fellow conspirators took down the economy of the former Soviet Union by collapsing its currency.

Whether in the past, or the present, conducting wars are a very expensive proposition. Governments often made attempts to create money to finance wars, but be it the Continental of the Revolutionary War or the Greenback of the Civil War, such promissory money was generally very poorly received by the public. This is where government partnership with those who can finance their escapades became so important and one of the primary roles played by the banking industry over the past several centuries.

Chapter 5 - Banking

Given the influence of money over man and of banking over money, it is understandable how the international banking powers have ultimately become deemed the modern day philosopher kings. Whether it is for individuals, nations, or operating internationally, banks function to hold our wealth, create our money, provide investment capital, issue our debt, etc. This was not always the case, for if you go back a couple centuries the "money changers" were considered lower echelon in society. This perspective was a resultant relic of church doctrine where usury laws were so strict, that only "the sinful" would engage in banking, thus relegated to Jews who were not under the authority of the church. Back in the time of Adam Smith, banking was established for public utility, rather than the powerful entity that controls such tremendous wealth today.

Prior to central banking, "free market" or independent banks were established, primarily as safe repositories for gold or other wealth. Notes of exchange were issued against deposits, which could then be used as currency. Even back in the late 1700's when "The Wealth of Nations" was published, what was termed "bank money" was valued at a premium over equivalent face note currency. These banks charged fees for their services, based on what the free market would bear. In time, banking evolved, whereby banks began to lend money against their deposits, from which it could charge interest and pay interest to depositors, rather than charging fees. Fractional banking followed, which allowed lending in excess of actual deposits, based on the assumption that not all notes of credit would be redeemed at once. This enabled significant growth in banking revenue, along with transaction fees based on free market conditions, up until the time when central banks came into existence.

The first central bank was the Bank of England, founded in 1694. It did not operate quite the same as central banks do today in that, like private banks, it issued currency redeemable against gold. Most other countries did not adopt permanent central banks until much later, generally in the late 19th and early 20th centuries. The first permanent U.S. central bank was established in 1913 and by the middle of the century, almost all nations had adopted central banking authorities.

The emergence of the central bank is generally attributed to power of the major banking dynasties, primarily with the Rothschild banking family in Europe and that of J.P. Morgan in the U.S. The Rothschild banking empire achieved such incredible success throughout Europe and became the leading lending partner to governments needing war financing. Similarly, J.P. Morgan (who was considered a U.S. Rothschild agent)[38] provided strong financial backing to the U.S. during the banking crisis of 1907, as well as financial support to U.S. allies in WWI. It was Morgan with the support of the international banking magnates and Washington insiders, who created the U.S. central bank, called the Federal Reserve. The plans were created at Morgan's island off the coast of Georgia, called Jekyll Island (thus named The Creature from Jekyll Island).[39]

Publicly, we are to believe that the role of the Federal Reserve, which is an independent agency despite the term "Federal", is to protect public welfare, by providing stability to financial markets as the lender of last resort, establishing monetary policy, provide banking oversight, issuing currency, etc. However, it is more likely that the true purpose of the Federal Reserve has more to do with preserving elitist economic gains of the top bankers and retaining and the political power structure they control. The Federal Reservist bankers have been given a monopoly position in lending money to the government and in return, the government is no longer required to rely on taxes and public support for waging wars and funding programs popular with its constituents. Treasury bond obligations can be sold to the public or to the Federal Reserve, who can use these obligations to create money. The public still pays the obligations with taxes and inflation, but they do not need to be consulted first. The government debt can also be used for redistribution, an important tool in moderating and controlling class warfare.

Formation of the central banks profoundly changed the free market. The exchange of gold and silver for bank notes, eventually gave way to notes that are now backed only by the guns of the government. Hard assets have since been converted to paper and digits. While the use value of gold and silver is still disputed, market value has been maintained relative to paper money. Even if Communist ideology

[38] G. Edward Griffin – The Creature from Jekyll Island
[39] ibid

were to prevail, the amount of labor required to secure these precious metals would still make them of significant value.

Most people think the Federal Reserve in the U.S. is controlled by the Federal Government, rather than an elitist private international banking monopoly. Central bankers now control the supply of our money, its cost to borrow, inflation, deflation, always guaranteed to stay ahead of economic upturns and downturns. They have a monopoly position to lend to the always ready to borrow Federal government, with interest of course. (Note that President Kennedy nominated an Executive Order to stop interest payments to the Federal Reserve prior to his assassination. The order died with Kennedy.) Such influence over macro economic trends and associated business cycles certainly facilitate insiders to optimize their personal fortunes in the most effective manner. But the true power is control of debt, which is the power to destroy the economies of any non-cooperative government.

Powerful politicians rely on the money suppliers as a source of political power. Perhaps the potential for abuse was best explained by one of the most astute statesmen in all of U.S. history, Thomas Jefferson, as noted in 1802:

'I believe that banking institutions are more dangerous to our liberties than standing armies. If the American people ever allow private banks to control the issue of their currency, first by inflation, then by deflation, the banks and corporations that will grow up around the banks will deprive the people of all property until their children wake-up homeless on the continent their fathers conquered....'

The international scene is much the same. The World Bank was formed following WWII and the Bretton Woods Agreements, which set up the IMF to manage balance of payments and to lend (taxpayer money) to poorer nations. It is not clear who benefitted from spreading this wealth, but criticism about misappropriation and misuse of funds for personal gains are common. Also out of Bretton Woods was the nomination of the U.S. dollar as the reserve currency, which at the time was pegged at $35 to the ounce of gold. This peg to gold was eliminated by President Nixon in 1971.

The truth is that the banks and multi-national corporations that have grown around them have generally replaced armies as the new vanguards of colonialism. Perhaps if any industry should be nationalized, banking may be it.

Chapter 6 - Gold and Money

Before leaving the topic of money, it is helpful to have at least some understanding of its origin and history. Throughout recorded history there are references to various types of money, i.e., something that either is of intrinsic value, or represents the promise to pay against something of value. For example, there were periods of time in our history when tobacco could be used as money. Though other commodities had been used as medium for exchange, as markets developed, the gold standard emerged as the free market medium of choice. While there are references to the use of gold as money in China dating back to 1100 B.C., I will restrict discussion to the current era.

The free market that began developing in the 17th century required a medium or standard by which trade value could be established. Although considered somewhat "mystical" by some, precious metals, particularly gold, became that medium most likely due to past history. Some important characteristics which influenced this free market choice of gold included the limits on the amount available, its ability to be weighed and assayed (difficulty to counterfeit), its durability, its ability to be coined and transported. Acceptance of the gold standard became international and for centuries it provided a sound basis by which money could be denominated against a certain weight of gold. Under gold standard money, there was much economic stability, i.e., no severe business cycles, with very limited inflation or deflation. This stability facilitated long term financial planning for individuals and businesses.

Many prominent economists still consider gold as a symbol of liberty given its link to the great civilizations built on the free gold standard. Other economists, such as British Fabianist (a socialist society) John Maynard Keynes, called it a "barbaric relic" and saw it as an impediment to economic development. Keynes will be discussed prominently throughout later chapters due to his highly accepted views on government interventionism. As the wars of the early 20th century, particularly WWI increased the need for government money, gold began to fall out of favor and countries began replacing it with fiat paper money. While for some time the paper money was still redeemable in gold (or in some cases silver), it eventually became disconnected from either. In 1933, confiscation of personal gold by the U.S. Government began to take place under the Trading with the Enemies Act, as it was labeled a "danger to society".

The confiscation of gold in favor of fiat money, which is backed by nothing, except the force of guns, is in the minds of many, an epoch change in modern political economy. The gold standard provided stable value to money and while it has been abolished as legal tender, continues to provide consistent purchasing power, while the value of fiat paper continues to be decimated. This is because the fiat paper money gets printed as needed out of Treasury debt to finance wars and welfare programs. Government deficit spending is unlimited as we now see in the U.S. (at $13 trillion) and the U.K. (currently at $12 trillion). This debt takes the form of Treasury bonds or can be monetized by the central banks by printing paper money.

As gold is basically indestructible, it continues to be accumulated rather than consumed. Total World stock of gold (production that remains either in circulation, in personal hands, or in reserves) is estimated (2000 figures) at about 4 billion ounces growing at about 2% annually.[40] While gold purchasing power has historically remained pretty consistent, it tends to spike in times of currency uncertainty. What better example than looking at the U.S. dollar price of gold with a historical price of $35/ounce in 1971 (the last year the US dollar was defined against gold for foreign markets and the official end of gold globally), to $375/ounce in 1995 to about $1400/ounce as of this writing. This foretells of a very high risk for our currency to be in crisis in the near term since changes in gold prices are now primarily a function of currency valuation.

The movement away from gold was preceded by a movement toward central banking and away from a free banking system. In addition to governments pushing for central banking, some religious groups also pushed for reforms to free banking system interest charges, advancing the cause of usury laws.

One might note that the word "Liberty" that appears on metal specie money (coinage), it has been removed from paper money. For many former holders of gold backed money, substituting "In God We Trust" on fiat currency was no replacement for "In Gold We Trust".

---

[40] Salsman, Richard M. Gold and Liberty. American Institute for Economic Research, 1995.

Once again, the invoking of the Divine is a great way to get public support behind a bad idea.

It would make for an interesting accounting to find where all the gold reserves are today.

Chapter 7 - Philosophical Views of Capitalism

There are some important philosophical principles that are inextricably connected with socialism and capitalism. Perhaps the most basic is that of private property. Capitalism is based on the principal of individual activities inspired to acquire property that can be claimed for oneself, while Communist ideology is based on the belief that the property of the Earth should be shared among its inhabitants "based on need". Communist ideology suggests that man does not possess inherent aggression toward others, but it is driven by pursuit of private property. Accordingly, enmity would disappear under Communism, because uneven advantage would be eliminated as would individual needs. This is counter to Freudian thinking, which suggests that we are not inherently friendly, but innately aggressive. Freud believed that natural individual differences in power and influence along with instinctive aggression supersede property ownership.[41] The second major ideological difference is that of free markets vs. State controlled markets. However, it is important to realize that most countries find some balance between the two structures, that no country operates in either purist form.

A key characteristic of capitalism is generation of profit. Most people in capitalistic society have a pretty good sense of what is profit, but as a very basic definition, it is the excess revenue after all expenses are covered. It is the primary goal of private and public corporations (excluding of course non-profits) and is the primary measure of success for most business. Winning in capitalism is all about finding a way to extract excess value, or profit from the system. Basically, this is about optimizing (maximizing) revenues and (minimizing) costs for the owners, be it private, or public enterprise. The profit motive has been blamed for many maladies of our society. This includes everything from the producing unhealthy foods we eat to drugs we take that are not designed to cure or prevent us from getting sick, but to keep us spending money on medications.

---

[41] Freud, Sigmund. Civilization and its Discontents.

Public corporations have an obligation to their owners to maximize long term profit, while individuals also pursue profit for themselves. From a philosophical standpoint, the question should be examined whether profit should be limited, or unlimited, under what circumstances, and how?

Looking deeper into capitalism in its purist form, we tout as its benefits a system that allows for free individual choice of vocation and presumably reward. On a macro level, the theory is that free and efficient markets will best deploy resources to meet overall needs and wants. An efficient capitalist market suggests market transparency, thus allowing supply and demand market dynamics to rapidly adjust. On a micro level, as suggested by early economic theorists such as Smith, even the self motivated gains will unintentionally promote the interests of the public. To illustrate this, Smith points out that individual capital employed for the greatest advantage infers that it will be applied in a way that maximizes exchangeable value. Therefore, an overall industry (for example in a producing country) is maximizing its value. Conversely, he believed that if something can be produced and supplied cheaper from elsewhere, it should be not be made locally.

As previously discussed, many economists believe free market capitalism contains the inherent ability to maintain the principles of supply and demand balance. As a macro sense example, a deflationary period caused by production oversupply will lead to production cuts, job cuts, decreased demand, which in turn drives down prices until excesses are cleared and equilibrium reestablished. Conversely, consumer demand for certain items will lead to higher prices followed by increased supply and ultimately reduced prices after supply catches up. Sometimes the balance will be overshot, and more production is needed to help off set the lower prices, therefore requiring expansion of markets to fend off a glut. From the consuming side of the equation, economic theory on consumer behavior suggests that consumers will constantly strive for higher quality, higher lifestyles, and will strive to maximize satisfaction based on budgetary constraints.

In terms of role and impact on the individual in the free market system, a person theoretically, should be aspiring to match their interests, level of challenge, and even political views with the right career choice. As such, many will end up in vocations that are much to their liking and some will even opt to continue working past their eligible retirement date. On the other hand, if someone aspires to a career for which there is no demand, they will likely have a difficult time meeting their needs. In reality, much of vocational choice is determined by market demand rather than individual preference.

This leads to an even more profound philosophical point; that most people have no idea what they really aspire to do with their lives other than pursue employment that will allow them to earn money. From an early age the preparation for vocation begins, through many years of schooling, training, and socializing. The truth is, without vocational and financial goals, most would not know what they would otherwise want to do. Unless, of course, you are born into fortunes that allow such freedoms of choice as to pursue a career, or just bum around the world, partying on your yacht, etc. From a humanistic perspective, would we actually prefer using our combined technological abilities to provide for everyone's basic needs and work to free our living hours from the labors and pursuit of money to pursue higher aspirations?

In addition, from a macro perspective, capitalism is a system based on competition…there are winners, there are losers. It is in a sense, economic Darwinism. Whether competition is fair or unfair depends upon one's perspective. What is now clear to most is that competition is driving everyone to work longer and harder, especially now that it is on a global basis and we are competing against others that have as much to gain as we have to lose. As competition continually increases, so does the stress and anxiety level in our society. It is no wonder that civility has decreased in our society despite being so heavily medicated. So the same force that continually drives improvements in all activities surrounding products and services, including innovation, technology, means of production, even in sports and entertainment, is the same force that enslaves us to continually needing to increase our own productivity and output. Since companies and individuals who have invested capital expect a return on that capital above simple interest, growth, or at least profit growth perpetuates this continuous process. This pursuit of ever increasing productivity can create a sense of increasing alienation from one's true passion as many become trapped by the fear of failure and the personal economic consequences of living in poverty. In addition, as people then compete to acquire scarce (in the economic sense) resources, the laws of supply and demand continually drive prices higher for those not keeping pace.

Finding the appropriate work/life balance has become increasingly difficult, as many people live for the weekends and a few weeks vacation each year, at best. Home ownership and affording at least some support toward higher education for their children is probably the gauge by which the majority of middle class will assess their economic success. Beyond that, affording decent end of life care will generally extract the majority of a life time of labor for the majority, with perhaps a small estate to pass along to the next generation. Perhaps one generation soon will finally say enough and decide they no longer want to play the game. Anecdotally, the growing nihilism would seem to suggest that this may be the case.

Another point of contention from capitalist critics connected with private property is the issue of inheritance. There is a saying that the most popular way to attain wealth (at least in our society) is the old fashion way…inherit it. This often includes many generations of "old" money, bearing the fruit of generations of others' labor, as invested capital must always produce a reasonable rate of return. In many cases, this wealth is actually pelf, originally obtained through ill gotten means, through the toil, sweat, and blood of the conquered. This seems especially true of the kings of enterprise created during the industrial revolution, with the backing of imperialistic governments. While there have been some outstanding philanthropic examples of successful capitalists in the past century and a half since the industrial revolution, most wealth gets passed down through inheritance from generation to generation among the elite. The substantial control over land, commodities, and commercial enterprise that became increasingly concentrated in the hands of the few lives on generation after generation, while the labor used to produce goods and their use value does not share in the rights to what is produced, but is exchanged for a wage controlled by the few.

On the other hand, there is no denying that free markets have rightly been credited with producing tremendous overall wealth and increased prosperity for many. One only needs to look at poverty statistics over the past couple centuries to today to see how the majority have come out of poverty. Under free market capitalism (before 1914) very large numbers of people escaped the lower working class into the middle and upper class, "with a standard of living exceeding the monarchs of previous ages" according to noted economist John Maynard Keynes. Private business ownership and public ownership of corporate stock allows many individuals to participate in the sharing of wealth generated by capitalistic businesses. So despite critic's claims that the prosperity tends to be highly concentrated, for example, in the U.S., the top 1% of the population controls 38% of the wealth, and the top 10%, control 74%, the non-wealthy appear to be better off than they were several generations ago. However, as all boats rise, increased demand for goods establishes new equilibriums which make achieving personal economic goals an elusive target for the majority.

So personal views on capitalism as a political economy will likely depend on how fairly one is being compensated, or perhaps to what ends the fruits of their labor go. Clearly, some get more than they rightfully earn while other share little for their efforts. This iniquity has been a point of contention since Aristotle, and probably throughout much of history. Adam Smith often harshly criticized those who act purely out of self-interest and greed, and warns that, "[a]ll for ourselves, and nothing for other people, seems, in every age of the world, to have been the vile maxim of the masters of mankind." (Book 3, Chapter 4)

Whether a disproportionate share of profit goes to highly compensated executives, large shareholders, bond holders, banks, politicians, etc., is a matter of perspective. But following the distribution of profit is "redistribution" which begins at the top in the form of business reinvestment, personal spending, exports to foreign markets, etc. It is by the spending of the rich and what the government redistributes from taxes for military, social services, infrastructure, debt service, etc., trickles down to the needy.

So aside from somewhat pervasive egoism, greed, and narcissism, the capitalist system works for most people, that is, most get enough out of the system to buy in. Whether this is because it truly is superior to socialism or it is because it has been marketed well by those it serves best is hard to say. Whether or not distraction by the various means of entertainment plays a significant role in anesthetizing the masses, is also contentious. One could speculate the reason for so much money in sports and entertainment, is that it plays the key role in as Plato put it "distracting us from the matters of the State." Be that as it may, provided people believe there is sufficient hope for as good or better life for their children and perhaps grandchildren, they are accepting of the system. Where confidence in the future is in peril, the working class becomes discontent. Debt is probably the greatest concern when it comes to future uncertainty as it has been such an important tool in keeping the whole system afloat. Before going on to a discussion on Socialism and Communism, it is worth a short look at debt in capitalistic society.

Chapter 8 - Role of Debt

The role of debt in capitalistic society is both important from a real economic sense and interesting from a philosophical sense. Such is its nature that the control and management of debt is an important topic of many religious texts. From a micro perspective, it plays a key role in personal finances, that which we as individuals incur to finance large purchases, such as homes, cars, higher education or even just general living expenses for those who use credit cards for such purposes. On a larger scale, there is business debt, such as bond issues to finance capital investments or for use in providing working capital when this can not be covered by current accounts or cash flows. On a grand scale is national debt, which the federal government uses to finance its operations, social programs, wars, etc. On a philosophical level, some would equate debt to slavery in that the debtor is beholden to the lender until such debt is repaid.

From one perspective, personal debt allows families to buy a home by way of a mortgage, to pay for a college education, both of which have longer term appreciation potential over the original value of the initial capital, and is therefore viewed as a positive element of debt. Savers can also be rewarded by lending their savings to potential borrowers via various money market instruments, thereby providing some gain on their savings. Likewise, corporate debt can be used for expanding a business enterprise beyond what can be financed through retained earnings in ways that provide a premium over the cost of the borrowed capital. Thus, managing the financial leverage of any given corporation is one of the primary tasks of its financial officers. Likewise, governments borrow money to pay for infrastructure projects, military operations, and finance general ongoing social obligations during times when these can not be covered by general tax revenues. While this topic alone has been studied in volumes, it will not be addressed in such great detail at this point, however, mechanisms of debt are worthy of some examination.

The advent of fractional reserve banking changed the complexion of debt in capitalistic economies. While the exact date of its origin is not clear, the practice started hundreds of years ago when banks began issuing both receipts for deposits and "duplicate" receipts to borrowers against those deposits. In a sense, there were now two claims against the same money, the lenders' and the borrowers', thereby expanding the actual money supply from debt. The practice eventually became widely accepted and now forms the basis of our current reserve banking system. Under the Federal Reserve, banks are given rules for how much money must be held in reserve, i.e., actually available against claims from depositors. Economic cycles are largely attributed to the expansion and contraction of money supply based on the reserve fractional banking systems. Another implication of the amount of money generated out of debt is the deflation of currency value, or conversely, continuous inflation of the goods which it purchases.

Government use of debt to finance wars and social programs must be balanced against the realities of revenue support. We are currently seeing the result of excessive social benefits in the sovereign debt crisis in Greece. The default on debt threatens the economies of Europe and beyond in this linked network of banking. Greek culture, while portrayed as one of humanistic, philosophic, and social disciplines, has been criticized in various media as "too humanistic" rather than fiscally conservative. There are reports that other Euro zone countries, such as Spain, Portugal and Ireland could be in similar danger of default. In one BBC report, allegations were made implying that foreign governments including the U.S. and U.K. were behind the over-blown financial crisis in order to improve the foreign market perceptions of their sovereign debt, which has been growing sharply. The U.S. and the U.K. are not without significant debt issues themselves, at $13 trillion and $12 trillion in federal government debt respectively. Thomas Jefferson made an interesting observation on the ongoing effects of national debt, "It is incumbent on every generation to pay its own debts as it goes. A principle which if acted on would save one-half the wars of the world." This link between wars, war debt, and banking are unmistakable and will be addressed later in greater detail.

Perhaps, as some fear, this growing debt will be a key factor in pushing nations in the direction of global crisis and ultimately global fascism. We seem to push forward, perhaps into oblivion, with enormous debt, perhaps all according to plan. In the U.S., we run trade deficits in the billions each month. To off set the imbalance, more money must be continually printed, which causes continual devaluation of our currency. Interestingly enough, it was Lenin who promoted the idea of "debauching currency as a means of destroying capitalism".

Chapter 9 – Socialism and Communism

I by no means profess an in depth understanding of Communism, nor will I attempt to provide anything other than a cursory explanation of how this political economy works within the context of this essay.

Even prior to the ushering in of the Industrial Revolution, there was considerable tension between the social classes. As the French writer Rousseau stated in his "Social Contract" in 1762, "Man is born free, and everywhere in chains", referring to the harsh conditions imposed on the working class. Inspired by the American Revolution, a movement to remove these chains grew strongest in France, with the French Revolution bringing euphoric results throughout Europe as a "regeneration of the human race." The European movement however, was not long lived, as it was eventually thwarted by the ruling aristocracy.

However, later in the century, as a counter cultural response to the ongoing conflicts spurred by imperialism, German philosopher Karl Marx, the father of the Communist movement, once again pressed for dramatic social change. Espousing the idea "from each according to his abilities, to each according to his needs", he published his Communist Manifesto, calling for "Working men of all countries, unite." Socialist philosophy sought to put an end to class struggle that existed throughout all of history caused by the exploitation of the dominant class against the dominated. The belief by Marx and others was that the dominant forces (bourgeoisie) had become so well entrenched, that there was no option for the dominated (proletariat) other then to unite and revolt. The mid nineteenth century when Marx, Engels, and others professed this new philosophy followed an intense period of consolidation of wealth and power created by the industrial revolution and imperialism, whereby powerful countries sought to expand trade and resource bases through military coercion.

This new ideology proposed that the resources of the world belong to all its inhabitants, thus there should be no rights to private property. Another key premise of this philosophy was that the value of commodity goods should be directly related to the amount of human labor input required for their acquisition or production.

While State control over productive resources seems to be anti-individual, it offers the advantage of focusing resources based on use value, rather than exchange value. Socialist philosophy was also touted as being freeing to man. When one considers how people spend so much of their human existence, energy, and focus on the pursuit of labor and vocation, the logic behind liberating people to pursue their real interests, seems obvious. For example, if someone wants to farm in the morning, fish in the afternoon, and maybe hunt the next day, they should be free to do so and to contribute to the overall social well being in a way that suits them best. When contrasted to the "mental mutilation" created by capitalistic division of labor, this certainly sounds preferable. Not only would a class less society free people from oppression, but Marx also believed that people would not need a formal government structure or army to control society. He proposed that after the proletariat took over, they could eventually eliminate formal government structure. Marxist philosophy also espoused anti-nationalism, since this was viewed as another means by the bourgeoisie to manipulate the proletariat. Production decisions for society would be democratically decided by the people. There would no longer be exploitation of one another. Success means that all boats are lifted, where in failure, all boats sink.

Despite Marxist ideological goals to free man, not all his ideals are viewed as necessarily liberating. Despite having some commonality with Christian teaching regarding common ownership, Marx was strongly against organized religion. Viewing religion, particularly Christianity as oppressive toward man's ability to fully develop and free himself, he believed it had no place in society. He saw religion as the "opiate of the masses", holding man down rather than elevating him to a higher calling. He also believed organized religion was just another part of the ruling class. So while ideologically in line with religious teaching on sharing, peace and non-oppression, this ideological divide would be become the lightning rod for anti-Communist agitators. It is more likely that this anti-religion aspect of the ideology created more opposition than its socioeconomic impact.

Outside influences over the ideology made it somewhat difficult to determine the original vision of the Communist movement, which was never really implemented in Russia. With U.S. and British backing, Lenin and Trotsky successfully defeated the true democratic revolution. Corruption, abuse and oppression replaced freedom. Like capitalistic society, elitists with the belief that people are not capable of governing themselves assumed control.

As an economic ideology, Communism has some shortcomings. While there could be an altruistic element that suggests society can be motivated for the greater good, many believe that people are much more motivated by self interests. Without the ability for one to get ahead, there is insufficient incentive to work hard, or take entrepreneurial risk. For the model to actually function, a society would either need to be "hard wired" to accept a "greater good" mentality, or require a societal programming, such as an indoctrinated idealism no different than that which drives our capitalist society.

While approximately 1/3 of the World was under Communist Control in 1980, most Westerners have a fairly limited understanding as to what Communism is about, only that it is our enemy. Aside from outright wars, there has been much transfer of wealth from richer to poorer nations that takes place behind the scenes, to "keep a country from becoming Communist, or from falling under terrorist control. Much of this comes from an unpublicized socialist effort to move money from the wealthier to poorer nations via the World Bank and in many cases investment by major corporations. The funding takes place without taxpayer consent, and whether or not it accomplishes altruistic humanitarian goals or whether it buys influence, loyalty and privilege for the elite in the recipient countries from the tyrants who run them, is a matter of opinion.

While concerted effort by capitalist powers worked successfully against the spread of the Communist model for many years, the emergence of Communist China as the worlds' economic tiger suggests at least a degree of merit to this political economic model. Founded in 1920, China holds the worlds' largest Communist party. In the West, we like to believe it was the opening of markets that made China the economic power house that it is today. While it is true that opening markets accelerated this growth, the foundations for organic growth from State investment in agricultural and industrial development had been taking hold. Western capitalists got into the act only after realizing that China had turned the corner and was rife for substantial GDP growth. An example of the financial support given to the burgeoning Chinese economy was the 1995 collaboration that took place between the Chinese State Planning Authorities and the World Bank. This involved development of project plans valued at $240B over 15 years to fund the building of energy infrastructure. As an illustration of China's economic success, their own published figures claim a reduction in poverty rates from 53% in 1985, to just 2.5% in 2005.

But the greatest change in the Communist world came with the collapse of the Soviet Union and with it, the diminished state control over many Eastern Bloc countries. It is not clear whether or not the collapse of Communism was due to failed ideology, or losing the battle against outside capitalistic influence. Many tend to believe the latter to be the true cause of failure. As some conspiracy theorists believe, the attacks of 9/11 may have been a cover up, targeting and destroying records that would prove covert funding of the final Soviet financial crisis.[42]

With the abundance of free flowing information now available from impartial sources over the internet, perhaps neither side now believes the lies that painted the other as evil. It is becoming clearer that there seems to be a movement of economic systems toward the middle. However, centuries of imperialistic wars over trade were required to get to this point and perhaps there are more yet to come.

---

[42] http://www.scribd.com/doc/4866520/Collateral-Damage-911-Covert-Ops-Funding-Targeted

Chapter 10 - Economics and Religion

No philosophical discussion on the societal merits of the various forms of political economy would be complete without at least incorporating some religious perspective. While volumes have been written on religious beliefs as they relate to economics, some of which I have captured previously, I will attempt to only make a few points.

Messages about wealth, its pursuit, and how it should be shared are prominent in all major religions and philosophies. Whether or not God plays or should play a role in political economy is somewhat moot, since both personal morality and laws governing economics and commerce have their basis in religious principles. In the U.S., we profess "In God we Trust" on our currency, but whether or not that has any meaning to those who control it seems doubtful, unless they consider themselves as God.

While perhaps somewhat archaic, there has been a historical view that the pursuit of wealth and riches are "evil". We have all heard how money (or the love of money) is the "root of all evil". Christian Gospels teach that it is "more difficult for a wealthy person to enter the Kingdom of God than for a camel to fit through an eye of a needle." Intuitively, we might expect most major religions to come down far toward the socialist perspective given alignment of socialist ideology with caring for others, versus capitalistic motivation driven by self interests. However, this is not necessarily the case.

While most religious leaders today tend to tread lightly on issues of political economy as "issues of the State", there are doctrinal guidelines spelled out for the faithful. An example of modern day Christian perspective is well described in an article by Professor Robert G. Kennedy, who believes that the Church has an ethical perspective that is much needed today. Seeking to combine the wisdom of the Church with the world of business, Kennedy teaches in the Department of Catholic Studies and the Department of Ethics and Business Law, at the University of St. Thomas in St. Paul, Minnesota.

Deeply embedded in the Catholic social tradition is the idea that the goods of the earth are intended to serve the welfare of all humanity. Pope John Paul II used to say that a "social mortgage was attached to all private property." This does not mean that individuals should not acquire wealth through their hard work and ability (which is a gift) but it does mean that God may call on them to use their wealth to help others.

In fact, Aquinas insisted that the natural purpose of excess wealth was to relieve the distress of the poor. The implication was not that it is the role or responsibility of government to determine excess wealth and to appropriate it. Instead, it is the duty of the wealthy to be moderate in their needs and to be prepared to use their abundance to serve those in need. If they fail to do this, Aquinas maintains, a person in great need may take what he requires for life and this taking is neither sinful nor theft.

The Marxist view is that private ownership is evil and the root cause of society ills. The Catholic view is that private property is a natural right, and respect for ownership is the best practical way to ensure that the goods of the earth are distributed properly. However, when some people are in distress, the wealthy become God's hands, so to speak, in serving the needs of the poor.[43]

Unfortunately, history suggests that the wealthy will generally not give up what they have willingly, and perpetual class struggle is our reality. The drive for private property drives evil behavior, wars, revolutions, and seemingly no chance for lasting peace.

Perhaps as some suggest, this constant struggle is a "natural" part of our human existence. It is part of the dualism of man, where we are always faced with choices between love and hate, war and peace, good and evil, life and death, truth and deception. Some believe that humanity can not really have one side without the other. As an example, if there is no one in need of mercy, there can be no mercy. This is somewhat connected with another school of philosophical thought common in the early 19th century, that through conflict mankind evolves toward its ultimate destiny. For if there is only agreement and complacency, there is no change. To illustrate, if Angels represent restraint, prudence, self doubt and lawfulness, Devils are then the inspired creators representing the opposite. Our human existence requires both the "Devourer and Prolific", which move us forward toward the end goal of humanity.

However, can it be a "natural" course in our history, the cycles of war and rebuilding, economic expansions and contractions, inflation

---

[43] The Ethics of Business

and deflation, or is it part of a control mechanism…particularly when both sides of a conflict have the same backer? Ultimately, it is through conflict that political, economic, and social systems are developed. With control over both sides of conflicts, there is always control over the outcome.

How should one judge those who horde wealth and power, good or evil? Certainly, manipulation and control by deceit of the majority of the earth's inhabitants, through fear, wars, and threat of punishment can only be evil. On the other one hand, exerting global control and distribution of resources may finally mark the end of man's historic conflict over control of the world's assets and productive capacity of its inhabitants.

Perhaps our "philosopher kings" can bring about a better result than any system run by the citizenry.

Chapter 11 - Normative Economics

In an effort to compensate for deficiencies inherent in capitalist free markets, normative economics is a branch of economics that addresses restoration of efficiency and fairness. It places value judgments on economic decisions and strives to create just public policy around these assessments. Government intervention in regulating and redistributing wealth is the primary driver behind normative changes.

Free market efficiency has long been a contentious point of debate among economists, since economic performance using indicators is not an exact science, subject to varying points of view. Early experts, like Adam Smith and even many today, believe that the "invisible hand" i.e., free market forces of supply and demand without government intervention, should drive economic decisions. While favoring this view, Smith was also an advocate for fairness, supporting taxes on the wealthy, support of education, and assistance to the poor. He was also a strong opponent of accumulated war debt being mortgaged against future generations. Perhaps the free hand would prove most effective, if not for the use of excessive debt as leverage to accelerate growth for the greedy and impatient.

There are a number of variations on free market economic thought. Renowned economist Jean Baptiste Say advocated savings as a means of investment. He also theorized that commodities can be produced to purchase other commodities; as such, there should never be a lack of money. He believed that supply and demand are always in balance, although misallocation can cause some markets to be short, while others long. Say advocated higher production to boost purchasing power, suggesting that production increases wealth, while consumption destroys it. The relationship between production output, labor and capital investment has been described by economists for many years (since the 1920's) using the Cobb-Douglas Production Function:

$$Q = aL^b \; K^{1-b} \quad \text{or alternately} \quad Q = aL^b \, K^c \quad \text{where } b+c \neq 1$$

where L is Labor and K is capital. Basically, this formula measures the marginal effect of Labor and Capital on output. Many arguments against the equation state that it neglects the effect of technology and management factors, which were later added in some forms of the equation. Ultimately, these equations have been used to define U.S. productive output, meaning we can put resources into labor, or capital to increase output. While a simple premise, it has importance when a government needs to weigh where to put stimulus depending upon unemployment rates, etc.

It was in the 1930's, that normative economics became popularized, most notably by British economist John Maynard Keynes. Keynesian Economics promotes government intervention in monetary policy to overcome market inefficiencies in strictly private sector economies. For example, economic stimulus can be applied to help increase demand that would not otherwise soak up excess supply (e.g., current housing crisis). This school of thought grew in popularity in the years that followed the Great Depression.

The cause of the Great Depression is still contentious, with the interventionist side laying blame on the gold standard, private banking abuses and other free market maladies, while the classic liberalists cite action by the government and the Federal Reserve as the cause. Regardless of the cause, the aftermath reaction from the Federal Government and the Federal Reserve resulted in a profound change to the U.S. free market and associated economic liberty. In 1931, the global economic system was in chaos, with the Bank of England in collapse as well as economic crises in Germany and Austria. The threat of a run on gold and reserves threatened collapse of interbank payments as the system was afloat on a sea of kited bills of exchange.[44] In order to stop the potential spread, a bail out fund of $125M was created by the reserve banks, administered by the National Credit Corporation.

In addition to bailouts, the government and Federal Reserve began assessing other ideas to stimulate economic growth in conjunction with private industry. Under Presidents Hoover and Roosevelt, and under the Federal Reserve direction of Eugene Meyer and later Marriner Eccles, various corporatist ideas, including suspension of certain anti-trust laws, financial support to selected growth industries (e.g. electrical products, primarily General Electric Corporation), reduced competition through preferential business

---

[44] Todd, Walker F. – The Federal Reserve Board and the Rise of the Corporate State 1931-1934. American Institute for Economic Research.

financing (stimulus) and intercession on establishing labor rates, were all in play to varying degrees. Influencing this initiative was the early success of the fascist Mussolini Italian government cooperating with private industry. Prior to this point, government intervention had been limited to protective tariffs.

There is still no clear decision as to whether the intervention action by the government and Federal Reserve led to a faster economic recovery. However, as pointed out by Walker Todd in his research, "private interests, acting through regional reserve banks, had made the system an ineffective instrument by which private interests alone could be served."[45] Government oversight, in conjunction with the activities of the Reconstruction Finance Corporation, ultimately led to greater consolidation and concentration of monetary power under the Federal Reserve.

Taxes are still the most powerful force in normative economics and redistribution of wealth. Whether used for public projects, military spending, or aid to foreign nations, they are a very powerful part of wealth redistribution. While Democrats and Republicans will fight over where the tax money goes and the varying degrees of redistribution of working class wealth, it is unlikely that those who reside at the top of the economic pyramid are affected by redistribution, as it would be foolish for those who make the rules to hurt themselves. As famously quoted many times, "taxes are for the little people." In reality, the class struggle that had taken place between the working and wealthy classes in the nineteenth and early twentieth centuries, has been cleverly shifted to become a conflict between the working and welfare class. Whether or not redistribution among the working and welfare class makes sense is a matter of opinion. As noted by Alan Greenspan prior to his appointment to the Federal Reserve, "it does not make sense to take from the productive to give to the unproductive." The ways in which government acts to allocate and redistribute wealth deserves further analysis.

---

[45] Ibid.

Chapter 12 - Government Roles, Guns and Butter

The role of government in U.S. political economy is one of ongoing controversy dating back to the writing of the Constitution. The initial role was quite limited, encompassing the levying of taxes and duties to provide for the defense and general welfare of the nation. The founders debated over the role of government money, whether to limit it to the minting of gold and silver coins, or to include issuance of government "bills of credit" should the government need to borrow. This was eventually clarified by James Madison in 1788, when he published in the Federalist that Constitutional authority was to establish monetary standards based on gold. Weights and measures were established in order to protect private property and prevent fraud.

The present role of government is considerably more active, and while maybe a bit cynical, it seems the primary role may be to preserve the political and economic gains of those who are truly in power. Preservation of power has been the primary goal of powerful governments throughout history. Dangers to those in power, those with the greatest at stake, can come from both outside forces and within a nation. This was the driver behind government and central banking partnership, where resource allocation can be used to head off potentially destabilizing problems. While we think of the management and allocation of national resources being conducted in full view of the public by our elected officials, the real social and economic policy decisions are made behind the scenes by those who we do not elect. Powerful individuals backed by large corporations and financial institutions operating in government advisory capacities, provide the proper guidance to politicians who do their bidding.

Particularly in military and non-domestic spending, there are many outside influences, as well as the input from U.S. intelligence agencies. Think tank groups such as the Council on Foreign Relations, Trilateral Commission, and the Bilderbergs, are among the very influential elitist advisory agencies.

U.S. foreign policy flexes our economic muscle across the globe. Foreign aid to allies or sanctions against non-cooperative governments provides powerful incentives for cooperation. Military response has become almost routine when sanctions fail. Some of these actions appear completely bereft of morality or conscious. Secret government agencies provide the intelligence to understand where threats to the current power structure come from, be it political instability, insurrection, ideological differences, etc. One of the primary roles of the CIA is the study and publication of economic data from around the world for use by those who control policy.

Other government agencies are focused on domestic stability, looking at any potential challenges to those in power from within. Controlling the collective ideology of the masses requires considerable understanding of the forces that motivate us, so that the appropriate stimulus can be provided to keep things on track. This assists in directing policy for wealth redistribution or other public programs important to maintaining the peace. In reality, there is really not much difference for most people who they elect to represent them. It is a false illusion of choice between liberals, conservatives, Democrats, and Republicans. While there are some differences in political positions, neither side will ever change the current true power structure that remains behind the scenes.

The balancing role the government and its puppeteers play between foreign and domestic issues can be described in terms of "Guns and Butter". Guns and Butter has been part of the economic vernacular since around the time of WWI, referring to a countries' decision on allocation of resources between military and civilian development.

Currently, the military is by far, the greatest U.S. welfare recipient, i.e., consuming the largest share of the Federal budget. The use of government funds for military purposes deserves much thought. Most view our historical military use as ideologically driven rather than politically and economically motivated and few would oppose a strong national defense. Vulnerability to foreign powers is inimical to self governance and freedom. On the other hand, the reality is that we have not used our military for defensive purposes since the attack on Pearl Harbor and this attack was both predictable and possibly avoidable. Our military is used almost exclusively for offensive purposes, despite those who claim these actions prevent conflict on home turf. Military spending has grown to astronomical proportions, with $800 B used for military operations in Iraq alone. While most people will likely never know the true motivation for this war, it is undeniable that there are those who made large fortunes in supplying the military industrial complex effort.

From an economic perspective, some consider military spending similar to other economic stimulus packages that go into public works (butter projects). They generate jobs, not just in the military, but also through the trickle down spending by defense contractors. Some see benefits in high tech R&D that yield future economic development, but it is unlikely military spending will improve national productive capacity and infrastructure that will lead to true job growth. For each very expensive bomb that is produced and exploded in a desert somewhere, there is no return on investment. Some military actions appear to be an intentionally wasteful use of resources, lacking any defined military objectives. With the expansive powers now given to the executive branch, particularly when it comes to waging war, we seem to be engaged in constant conflict. Some attribute this as the responsible role of the world's last remaining super power. While other nations, Germany for example, vanquished in the World Wars, is no longer required to use substantial national resources on military spending. As such, they have had great financial success in building infrastructure for industrial economic expansion.

There are some financial winners when it comes to war. Governments use debt to finance very high cost wars, creating large sums of money, which gets circulated through the military industrial complex. Thus, in a sense, wars actually create more money as economic stimulus. The lenders of the money, created out of nothing, but bearing interest are obvious beneficiaries, along with the military contractors and companies involved in all the rebuilding that takes place from war's destruction.

There is always "trickle down" from government spending, but the closest to the printing presses get the greatest benefit. As the money circulates through the economy and purchases more goods and services, the benefit decreases as inflated demand has decreased or diluted the value of the money. The closest to the printing presses get the most benefit, but the trickle down touches many.

The "Butter" side of government spending gained notoriety in the post Depression Roosevelt era but has made a great resurgence today with the American Recovery Act. Infrastructure projects are providing some employment while we wait for normative forces to restore the appropriate balance caused by bursting of credit market bubbles and the move of production jobs overseas. Time will tell whether we can keep the printing presses running long enough for this to happen.

When it comes to spending on public welfare, there is no bigger issue than that of government sponsored health care. The government take over of health care poses some interesting questions and speculation. It is unlikely that they will reveal the true impetus behind the takeover, nor all the hidden agenda items within the more than 1000 pages of legislation. The government assertion that this is necessary to stave off further economic crises due to escalation of costs is probably not true. Many rightfully fear that this is the beginning of a new American socialism as the government looks to control an industry that makes up 1/3 of our GDP. From an economic liberalist perspective, it is a huge step in interventionalist government, and brings with it the associated loss of personal liberty. Others fear there will be government rationalization of health care.

Despite objections by some individuals and small business, large corporations who foot the major share of the health care costs for their employees are probably relieved to have the government take over the system in order to mitigate economic uncertainty due to escalating provider costs. It is the same rationale drove most companies to abandon their pension plans. The unpredictability of pension plan investment performance was a problem for corporations, so most enhanced employee's savings plans and shifted the uncertainty of performance to the employee.

But there seems to be a broader ideological basis for the change. The rationale for changing the system is not about the 30 million uninsured, when it includes hundreds of millions who are insured. The other questionable aspect of the government take over is where will the savings come from? Will health care professionals lose jobs, or get paid less? Will it exacerbate the already high unemployment problem? One of the more difficult points to reconcile in the health care debate is that most feel we have the best system in the world. It functions for the vast majority and yet, it will be changed for everyone, not just those who do not have access. There is no "opt out" provision and funding has not been defined.

Yet, in conversations with associates from outside the U.S., the general consensus is that they think it unconscionable that Americans would not support universal health care in a nation so strong and prosperous. Perhaps they are correct, or maybe this is just another step in globalization, aligning us more closely with other nations as we approach the capitalist/socialist synthesis. One thing for certain, the role and control of central government and its allies continues to strengthen. With complete access to our personal records, requirement of national I.D.'s and maybe the eventual rationing of care, we are certainly heading away from the path of liberty and freedom.

Taking the health care issue a step forward, if it is a good idea because we all need health care, maybe central government should take over providing our food and housing since we all need that too. It is certainly not a stretch that education, including higher education should be a public right, provided by the government. Maybe insurance, banking, or even taking over the issuance of our money from the Federal Reserve could be next. In any case, government insiders, those closest to the printing presses as payments come out, will get the most benefit.

Perhaps the government can manage health care by turning it into a mountain of debt, the same way social security has been managed....simply add it to the unfunded liability debt heap. In the meantime, the impact of all the deficit spending on our hard earned and harder saved dollars is evident. The U.S. Dollar has plunged in value against gold, from about 1/400 per ounce of gold to about 1/1400 per ounce in just a few short years. It is not just gold, as we see rising oil prices again approaching the $100/barrel level. While some may argue that a supply / demand imbalance for these commodities is the driving force behind the escalating prices, this does not explain the 75% drop against the yen over the past 40 years, or the 30% drop against the Euro this decade.

So the real key for those who control our financial resources is to find the right balance between Guns and Butter spending, to appease those who keep them in office.

Chapter 13 - What Do We Really Want Out of an Economic System?

Perhaps this is the real question we should be asking ourselves. Although, very few people understand who really controls international political economy let alone have any influence over it. Even control of our own economy remains a mystery to most. For example, most people seem to think the Federal Reserve is part of the Federal Government, not understanding, it is a private banking entity. In truth, political economy has much more control over us than we have over it.

If working class citizens of the U.S. were given a chance to restructure our economic system, what might it look like? Would we change anything, maybe attempting to make it freer or fairer? We could go back to Classic liberalism, the non-interventionist free market system, or further toward Keynesianism, with greater central planning and intervention to influence markets. We could try areas in between, such as the less known corporatism, which organizes society on the basis of professional or occupational "chambers" designed to help manage class conflict. This school of thought is believed to have its origins in Catholic social teaching of 19th century France and Italy. Some might suggest something real radical; use our technological know how toward developing a political economy with a goal of minimizing human suffering globally.

While the free market has allowed so many to achieve tremendous economic success, it has had some less than desirable consequences as well. Aside from the abuses of labor at the hands of the wealthy, there are flagrant financial abuses, such as excessive bonuses and parachute packages for non-deserving managers, particularly those associated with Wall Street. These bonuses must come from somewhere, generally inflated prices on products and services purchased by the masses. Consider as an example a home heating oil company that must add $0.40/gallon to your oil bill to pay for hedging. Then we read that the average pay for the top 20 hedge fund managers in 2009 was $600M, with several exceeding $1B. It is no wonder we have not graduated past the class struggle that has plagued humankind throughout history when such greed persists. In reality, this activity adds much cost but brings no social value.

Obviously, freedom in economic systems requires moderation and temperance to work.

Another great obstacle a free system has to overcoming class struggle is the inheritance system. Inheritance is still the most popular route to obtaining wealth and it becomes even more unjust where the "old money" has less than honorable origins, i.e., pelf. Even free market advocate Adam Smith wrote in opposition of perpetuating land ownership from generation to generation. With a sound economic starting point, one merely needs to make reasonable investments to appreciate his capital position. It is possible for generation upon generation of people who do not actually "do" anything to contribute to society, other than rely on the labor of others to grow their wealth. Particularly in cases of illicit financial gains, should there be a limit on inheritance? An egalitarian view would suggest that we all start from the same ground.

Conversely, we have not necessarily faired that well under Keynesian government and central banking intervention. While the welfare class and perhaps lower working class may have improved their lot, there has been considerable loss of liberty for all citizens. The masses have also had to accept constant war, inflation, erratic business cycles and a government that operates largely in secrecy. Workers seem destined to bear the financial yoke of military adventurism, welfare statism, endless wars and debt.

In any case, it is uncertain that what has worked in the past will work in the future. In order to determine a reasonable path forward, it probably makes sense to look retrospectively at what has worked well to this point and what will likely need to be changed. Rapid economic growth, with associated real returns (above inflation), were rather easily attainable given the tremendous historical population growth. Considering that global population grew from about 1 billion in 1800 to 6 billion in 2000, it is easy to understand the driver of demand growth. However, things are changing with increasing concern over global overpopulation. Poor education of women, lack of women's rights, poverty and inadequate education in family planning are cited by our global population experts as primary causes. Despite these concerns over population, scarcity of resources, global energy shortages, global warming, etc., many developed nations are in population decline. For example, according to published figures, a nation needs a fertility rate of 2.1 children per woman to keep population from falling. Rates for a number of Western nations include Italy at 1.2, Germany at 1.3, Russia at 1.35, Japan at 1.43, and the U.S. at 1.99.[46]

Immigration is often the means to combat the shortfall from low birth rate and to help maintain balance between the working and aging. In the U.S., we have allowed the large "illegal" immigration from Mexico to help restore demographic balance, with the younger immigrants needed to help pay for the aging population. Flat population growth also explains the impetus to develop business in China, home to 20% of the global population. With flat to declining population in much of the developed economies, profitable growth, (or stage four economics) is increasingly difficult except in those areas where the standard of living is on the increase, e.g. Asia and Latin America. Without this growth, maintaining profit in mature markets is largely driven by consolidation.

So we are faced with the ongoing challenge of providing economic growth against adverse factors. Economic growth is really about the acceleration of capital. It is fueled by population growth, expanded markets, increased consumption and productivity enhancements. But the ongoing need for increased profits that continues to drive higher productivity also eliminates jobs for workers and purchasing power. This in turn, drives individuals toward pursuit of higher skilled positions, requiring higher education, pressuring greater academic competition, and so on.

Perhaps with the nature of global change, the depletion of natural resources, the pressure to decrease population growth, the redistribution of wealth and the decrease in poverty throughout the world, is the capitalistic system headed for failure? Since it is a system that survives on growth, i.e., the continual return on invested capital, will it reach a point where required growth is no longer sustainable? One could also surmise that if needs are increasingly met throughout the world and there is no population growth, considerable economic slow down will take place. In turn, this will further eliminate jobs, reduced demand, and decrease investment, until an overall lower standard of living is achieved where the supply and demand system rebalances or massive debt default causes more calamitous economic implosion. Perhaps consumer burnout in the pursuit of bigger and better materialistic goods will play itself out and people look toward other means of fulfillment in spending their time and effort.

---

[46] International Marketing, reprinted from "Population Shortfalls", Washington Post, April 3, 2000 by Bruce Bartlett.

This may not be altogether a bad thing. With work no longer a means to an end, it has become the end as people have lost connection with their natural being under serfdom. We are all highly engaged in an endeavor, but no one real knows to what end. Whether or not there is a systemic economic problem is probably a matter of one's own perspective…if one feels they are ahead of the game, there is no problem, where as if one is not reaping adequate benefit or making ends meet, the system is broken.   Nothing blinds a person to shortcomings of a system like financial success.

One has to assume that those who control the economic direction of international economies are already anticipating the need for change. There is ample evidence to suggest we are moving toward a "synthesis" global system based on the pure capitalist (thesis) and pure socialist (antithesis). Many European countries and Canada have moved toward this "hybrid" model, which provides varying levels of State direction and ownership in companies, higher taxes to support the general welfare of society, and a lower spread in income level between executives and labor. In the U.S., our economy is far toward the free market as opposed to a social democracy, even though we have public funded schools, a central bank, postal service, law enforcement, Medicare, and numerous government agencies. We see increasing evidence with government intervention, stimulus, and health care, that we are moving further toward a more socialistic "synthesis". In the U.S. people are taking sides on which direction things should head, be it resistance to or embracing greater socialist influence. But continued economic downturn will likely move things in the socialistic direction as more people need increasingly greater government support.

However, capitalism is highly engrained in our culture. Our unique needs and wants are part of our individualism and optimism has always led many to believe they can achieve a high level of economic success. We would be reluctant to accept that a home, educational opportunities, decent health care, etc., is everything we need. But at some point, the majority may conclude that work life balance is more important than maximizing wealth. With high unemployment giving employers a sustained upper hand and requiring employee concessions, more may perceive free enterprise as abusive versus fair. We know by laws of supply and demand, that essentially, we are competing against one another in an endless struggle that creates inflation, thus to the detriment of anyone who does not keep pace. People may eventually grow weary of this struggle against one another, especially as global competition continues to increase.

If we are heading toward a change, one that incorporates free market characteristics with socialism, the societal changes that take place could prove very interesting. As an example, if there is an economic "reboot" would the issue of fairness in compensation come under consideration? If so, then defining what is fair becomes a daunting challenge…is it compensation based on level of self alienation, benefit to society, dictated by whom, etc. One could imagine a grading system that considers skill level, quantity of labor, benefit to society, creativity, supply, degree of alienation, time, etc. as elements of the formula.

Could inheritance and trust funds be on the table? Certainly, we do not start life on an equal playing field, which suggests unfairness. Upper limits on income, which could be imposed as a 100% tax above income after a certain level, could become a reality. Philosophically, the idea is not without some merit. As much as some people would defend those making $50M, $200M or $1B in a year, one could also make arguments against it being in the public interest. Perhaps an asset tax which gradually increases based on value of holdings would limit extreme wealth accumulation. This would prevent dangerous accumulation of wealth and power, while keeping money circulating instead of potential hoarding. Of course, any such major change can be perilous, with possible adverse impacts on funds available for investment required to facilitate corporate and personal growth through equity and loan financing. Limitations on certain investment vehicles, e.g., options and derivatives might also be considered on the basis of whether or not they bring value to society.

Would such changes that ultimately make us all somewhat financially poorer be worth it? While difficult to say, the division of labor and self alienation driven by ever increasing competition no longer allows us to conceive what it would be like to be free of it. Not only have we lost ourselves as individuals, but as a society in whole. This is not to say all have been alienated, as some have found labors of love and others have managed to maintain simple lifestyles that only require limited personal energy and alienation. But for so many, personal character is defined by their competitive materialistic pursuits and their work that is the culmination of all physical and mental energies. The standard 40 hour work week has drifted to 50 and 60 hours or more for so many trapped in this endeavor. Probably the most interesting societal changes would be how people might respond to greater freedom of their time and energy. Would it lead to greater spirituality, closer families, pursuit of arts and literature, or more mind numbing entertainment and narcissism?

Chapter 14 - Current Economic Crisis

Never let a good crisis go to waste, especially if you go through all the trouble to intentionally create it. Reminiscent of past economic crises, most notably the Great Depression, this current crisis is indicative of a recurring problem of mismanaged financial policy (or cleverly managed policy, depending on your view) by governments and central banking authorities.

Not unlike economic crises of the past, the financial crises in which we now find ourselves, was created by the cycling of money supply by the Federal Reserve and other central banks with the associated formation and bursting of bubbles thus created. How this was done seems pretty evident to most...extremely loose monetary policy with artificially low interest rates, low reserve rates, plenty of money for everyone. The end result was easily predictable, as even a layman such as I had no trouble seeing this coming. Just as the Federal Reserve sets interest rates and reserve rates in the U.S., other central banks elsewhere function similarly.

In the U.S., government agencies also played a key role, enacting regulations designed to ease mortgage lending standards to encourage people who could not afford homes to buy them. Banks jumped in with both feet, but why not...they could bundle mortgages for the investment community and the very large banks can always get bailed out by the taxpayers. So with the great spending binge we end up with tremendous asset bubbles, particularly in the housing market, that once pricked, starts the chain of defaults. As consumers, we got sucked in, with easy credit, house appreciation that was like having a built in ATM, in addition to benefitting from the trickle down generated by so much spending. While the overall economy benefitted given the acceleration of capital generated by easy credit, most people did not plan on the party ending, and got stuck in a major deleveraging hangover.

The U.S. economy is estimated to be 80% driven by consumer spending, which really means those who hold the money, need to spend it so it can accelerate through the economic system. With concern created over burst asset bubbles, consumer spending dropped.

Businesses do not expand, capital does not flow from investors into commercial markets, but seeks safe haven in lower return fixed investments, such as treasuries. Other investors sought the security of gold. While I predicted a very strong run up in the value of gold, I was surprised at how its value increased over 300% in just a few years. On the other hand, the sharp rise in gold prices is a definite indication in the lack of confidence in our currency. Typically, rising gold prices are indicative of high periods of inflation ahead, higher interest rates (to cover the decreasing future value of money), and decreasing bond prices. Tangible assets tend to increase in price and corporate profits will likely decline.[47]

In a sense, you get a hoarding of money by the wealthy. This is a natural consequence as investment goals are always to return a risk premium on capital invested, that is, compensation over a guaranteed return commensurate with risk. The ripple effect is of course, high unemployment, poor returns on investments, and significant increase in government debt to stimulate growth.

Unfortunately, unless you are on the inside, it is hard to understand why crises are created, but perhaps it will become clearer as it unfolds globally. However, whether economies experience tremendous growth or calamitous decline, the opportunity to capitalize and expand ones own holdings is there if you know which direction things will take. For those on the inside, this is always the case, since it is within their control. The profit potential for insiders, heavily invested during expansion, and bailing out at the top, leaving borrowers, uniformed investors and taxpayers holding the over inflated asset bag, is tremendous. In addition, when everything crashes, they can pick up distressed assets at bargain prices. This was believed to be the case following the Great Depression.

While major corporations take a big hit in profits, there are longer term benefits for the well connected. Consolidation through continuous buyouts is facilitated when valuations drop, creating strong longer term growth while removing some competition. There are also gains realized by reducing employee salary and benefit costs, as fear of job loss in a bad economy is a great motivator. People in fear of losing their jobs will be willing to work harder and accept less, i.e., no raises, elimination of pensions, less benefits, etc. Unfortunately many in the workforce who expected to retire soon, lost so much value in their

---

[47] Gold and Liberty.

retirement savings, the thought of retirement and freedom has disappeared.

Adding insult to injury the banks, which despite bearing much of the blame for reckless lending practices, are taking advantage of high government debt and low Fed funds rates by engaging in carry trade. With Federal Funds rates near zero, they can take borrowed money, lend it to the government at a higher interest rate, who can than sell treasuries to investors, all subsidized by the taxpayer. This is preferred to lending it to individuals and businesses, even though taxpayers fund the bailout for these same banks that were "too large to fail".

Speculation about the real drivers behind the economic crisis varies, with some believing it may have more to do with macro economic adjustments rather than personal gain for insiders. In one school of thought, the crisis is used to "downward adjust" the relative wealth for a large segment of middle class, which had grown substantially in terms of real estate equity and retirement portfolios. The collapse provides considerable readjustment in middle class wealth distribution, closing the gap for the non-homeowner lower middle and younger middle classes, who were becoming relatively poorer. Another theory is that the prolonged period of economic expansion facilitated accelerated capital outflows to growth markets, such as China. Readily available low cost money provided a longer term high growth opportunity for those who were in a position to capitalize on foreign investment.

However, prevailing thought among many conspiracy theorists is that it is just another step toward implementing global economic consolidation. Globalization and building a New World Order has been the elitist agenda for a century, maybe longer. Controlling only certain national economies is not enough. It is at least anecdotally evident that strategists have been working toward this global goal, organizing industry in geographic areas of specialization to optimize production and presumably, profitability. Transference of wealth from wealthier Western nations to poorer countries has been part of the formula. Some speculate that once all the major economies are adequately connected, a global economic crisis will be used to consolidate financial authority through a common financial entity and common currency. In a sense, it would work the same way our Federal Reserve was created, in wake of what is believed by many to be a concocted financial crisis, but this time it would take place globally.

Whether or not the current financial crisis was created deliberately based of ideological goals, a result of incompetence or greed, we may never know. Most people can only contend with what is relevant to them, i.e., depreciated asset values and high unemployment. While there has been a great deal of success in raising the income levels in regions receiving capital inflows, generating demand and spurring economic growth, it will take many years for this growth to produce sufficient trade opportunities to off set the high local job losses. Critical mass to effectively compete in the global market place has lead to consolidation and acquisition activities of companies in every major industrial category.

While many politicians are probably well intentioned in efforts to provide better economic opportunities, they are simply not capable of offering much help.   This is because the real power is controlled by central banks, major corporations and a few well connected government insiders. Aside from establishing monetary policy, and printing money, the Federal Reserve also has the responsibility to generate and publish a host of national financial data. Figures can be manipulated and can be misleading. For example inflation rates tend to be misleading as they are generally expressed in terms of core inflation, which takes out food and energy (basic needs). The CIA also plays a major role in providing economic data to the monetary controlling body, publishing global figures on economic development, GDP, etc.

Politicians are heavily promoting the growth of small business. The government push for small business lending suggests a reliance on small business to be the engine for job growth.   Perhaps there are opportunities out there, but for the most part, without population growth or growth around new technologies, there is not much low hanging fruit for entrepreneurs. We can't all make a living in small retail.   It will undoubtedly take time to replace all the lost manufacturing opportunities from exported industries, with now only 10% of Americans actually employed in the manufacturing of a material product.

The lack of jobs, longer hours for those who have them, higher national debt, and prospects of higher taxes and fewer services, will continue to create stress in our society. Hopefully, corrective measures will take place before tension becomes unrest. It has always been the case in history, that the hungry are not peaceful. Whether economic stimulus and infrastructure projects can take up the slack while we wait for developing nations rise to a point where they generate equilibrium trade opportunities remains to be seen. More likely, they are a short term placebo creating road work jobs that will not have long term economic benefit, but will help assure economic destruction created through the amassing of mountains of debt.

Stimulus programs, wars, and promotion of small business will not make up for the job losses from efficiency gains and export of manufacturing. This leaves us without enough jobs, therefore, without money, and unable to meet needs and wants.

Conclusion

So where does all this leave us as individuals, as a nation, and as a global community? What should be our expectations for the future? Starting with the big picture, we are now part of global economy with a GDP of about $58T according to figures by the IMF, CIA and World Bank. The per capita GWP in 2008 was approximately $10,500 U.S. dollars.

To put this into some historical perspective, J. Bradford DeLong of the Department of Economics, U.C. Berkeley has estimated Total World GDP for the period one million BC to 2000 AD. Rather than reproduce the entire period, the last millennium has been published below.[48] Figures are in Billions, where 'Billion' in the table below refers to the American usage of the term, i.e. the short scale, '1 billion = 1000 millions = 10^9'.

1000 AD	35.31
1100 AD	39.60
1200 AD	37.44
1250 AD	35.58
1300 AD	32.09
1340 AD	40.50
1400 AD	44.92
1500 AD	58.67
1600 AD	77.01
1650 AD	81.74

---

[48]http://econ161.berkeley.edu/TCEH/1998_Draft/World_GDP/Estimating_World_GDP.html Estimating World GDP, One Million B.C. - Present

1700 AD	99.80
1750 AD	128.51
1800 AD	175.24
1850 AD	359.90
1875 AD	568.08
1900 AD	1102.96
1920 AD	1733.67
1925 AD	2102.88
1930 AD	2253.81
1940 AD	3001.36
1950 AD	4081.81
1955 AD	5430.44
1960 AD	6855.25
1965 AD	9126.98
1970 AD	12137.94
1975 AD	15149.42
1980 AD	18818.46
1985 AD	22481.11
1990 AD	27539.57
1995 AD	33644.33
2000 AD	41016.69

As noted, DeLong included statistics going all the way back to 1,000,000 BC (estimated at 0.01B). As an interesting note, his data revealed global GDP tripling in the millennium from 1000 BC to 1 AD from approximately 6 to 18 billion and roughly doubling again in the next millennium from 1 AD to 1000 AD. In the millennium included above, there has been more than one thousand fold growth of GDP, particularly from the mid 1700's on where population and GDP soared.

Perhaps these figures are only somewhat relevant, as they are simply digits and one can not necessarily relate this to any standard of wealth or well being. However, it does clearly indicate tremendous change brought about by the cumulative productive activities of mankind and his prevailing political economy.

Individual national wealth statistics published by the CIA are also interesting, but can be misleading without proper interpretation. For example, when we hear about countries where average annual incomes are $1,000 or less, we might assume abject poverty. However, this needs to be related to the cost of goods in that country, so the CIA and other agencies generally normalize data using purchasing power parity (PPP) which is a truer measure in terms of relative wealth.

With regard to population, according to recent CIA data, global population is currently growing by about 80M people per year, despite considerably lower birth rates. Better health care and healthier life styles are contributing to the growth. While population growth was once the driver of prosperity, population control is now the mantra of the "informed", with the Chinese model of government enforced population control gaining popularity among many of the elitist thinkers. Strain on food, energy, clean water and other resources along with global climate change now weighs heavily on the collective psyche of advanced nations as a real threat to the status quo.

There are some interesting but perhaps alarming statistics about wealth distribution in our U.S. economy. For example, the top 10% control 71% of U.S. wealth, with the top 1% controlling 38%. The disparity leads to some obvious class struggle issues and suggests that we could be on a collision course between the "haves" and "have nots", and those who support and oppose redistribution. While global statistics were not available, one can assume they likely look worse. It is also worth noting that less than 10% of Americans are actually employed in the manufacturing of a product. The lack of manufacturing is a significant contributing factor to our huge trade imbalances, now over $700B annually, over half of which is with China. It was trade imbalances that likely forced the permanent abandonment of the gold standard in the 1970's so money could be more readily printed to cover the imbalances.

Popular belief is that "high priced U.S. labor" caused the demise of our manufacturing industry. This is probably not true, although the occasional abuse of labor unions is a secondary factor for the change. The most obvious driver was the opportunity for much greater returns on investment, given the enormity of the Chinese market potential. Inexpensive plants constructed using low cost labor, less stringent engineering and environmental standards, and with subsidies from the Chinese government, who is also part owner, fueled explosive growth in new plants with low capital structure. Financial assistance from the international banking community (including loans that were subsidized by taxpayers) served to buy influence for those inside financiers.

While the consumer benefits short term from the very inexpensive subsidized products, this will change as domestic Chinese demand increases and dollar purchasing power decreases. When this happens, consumers will face noticeable inflation, compounding the high unemployment problem caused by the loss of their manufacturing jobs. Increased demand will also continue to strain global resources, especially energy. Ultimately this situation has the potential to erode far enough to cause debt default and perhaps worse economic calamity.

While financial return may be the obvious reason for the high Chinese investment, there could be underlying motives. With China poised for economic success prior to the large influx of Western capital, it is possible that the only way to prevent the world from witnessing a successful Communist economic model was through intervention. While Western capitalists defeated the Soviet Union in the economic Cold War, they were not likely able to wage an effective war in the same way against China. By engaging in China's economic success, they are effectively gaining at least some level of control in it.

In addition, competition from China and India are being used as the competitive hammer to motivate Western workers. This is a good example of playing both sides, as the competition is sponsored by the same banks, multi-national corporations and governments, who invest, subsidize and create labor standards to provide the right competitive environment. Perhaps spreading wealth to poorer nations through investment is morally just, if it were to benefit the people of the receiving nation. However, once the competition is up to speed, labor laws, environmental standards, subsidies and wealth redistribution can once again rebalance the playing field and investments will probably go to the next cheapest labor pool. As long as everyone keeps working harder, with producers and investors maximizing profits, the system is working.

So where does this leave the average worker? Many will continue the delusion that the system works and we control our economic destiny unless or until things go terribly wrong. Most will not acknowledge the reality that the system is manipulated by the few as most are completely apathetic to the process. More young people will enter college with the hopes that a degree will provide the needed competitive edge, only to learn that the competitive bar has again been raised. They will end up accepting employment that lacks the mental stimulation and financial rewards they expected. Particularly, with the increasing division of labor, monotony is the enemy of many educated laborers. It is a reasonable explanation for the widespread distraction with television, drugs, and alcohol that continue to anesthetize the masses. Perhaps the pursuit of new technology will generate new opportunities, but the continued de-emphasis of humanistic thinking creates other societal health concerns.

Perhaps one positive sign is that younger workers seem to be more inclined toward quality of life pursuits, which include increased leisure time, versus strictly materialistic pursuits. Vacations, leisure activities, quality of life goods and services, will likely remain in high demand in the coming years. On the other hand, some social critics believe there is an alarming trend toward an increasingly nihilistic view of our economy resulting from the mountains of debt and inequities created by capitalist greed.

As a nation, we have a lot to contend with. While increased involvement in the international business environment provides tremendous opportunity to help create peace through mutual understanding and interdependencies, we fail to find much common ground on domestic economic issues. We are highly polarized in views on government redistribution policies and face a worsening class conflict. Our acrimonious politics includes on one side, proponents of a greater role in government redistribution of wealth through various stimuli, health care and other social programs. On the other end of the spectrum is the "Tea Party" who fights against government intervention and increased taxes represented by this redistribution. To some degree, both sides should be admired for their efforts in trying to make a difference, although it is unlikely either side will be successful in achieving their goals. One solution may be to go the way of the former Soviet Union. We could possibly decentralize federal government power to give much more authority to the states. A weaker federal government would allow people gravitate toward states that adopt ideologies more in line with their own. While this idea may have merit, I suspect those in power would be strongly opposed and they control the military. Breakaway attempts would likely end up with similar results as the Civil War, or on a smaller scale, the Branch Davidians.

It seems that no matter what we do to influence the economy, we are always dealing with trade offs. Industrial growth consumes limited energy resources and creates environmental concerns, increased savings causes economic slow downs, increased spending reduces savings and investment rates, economic growth and higher wages causes inflation, increased capital expenditures for productivity reduces jobs... recession, inflation, supply, demand, needs, wants, we seem to be in a zero sum game. It is as if we are trapped in a perfectly well constructed enigma with the iniquities of both the right and left, socialist and capitalist always battling in the forefront of our politics. It is likely the beaten down populace will ultimately succumb to an eventual synthesis rather than thinking outside the box, where perhaps the best solution lies.

Life, Liberty, and the Pursuit of Happiness are becoming ephemeral illusions of freedom held in the past. Here in the U.S. we proclaim to be the vanguards of freedom, but we use our military around the world to impose our materialistic variety of freedom while armies of militarized police at home keep us free from our own devices. Positive change is not likely going to happen by rotating politicians, but will need to come from those who set the agendas and ideologies for the politicians from behind the scenes.

Whether peaceful solutions to economic inequality will ever be found, is difficult to say. Maybe the problem has been going on forever, even as Adam Smith wrote in the 1700's of the "violence and injustice of the rulers of mankind as an ancient evil".

While we may be able to secure for ourselves a level of peace through financial security, but we will never really have true peace where there is hunger, oppression, and living in fear. There needs to be a least a level of security to support basic freedom. The poor can be oppressed, wealth defended, but there will never be peace without justice.

Whether the current economic crisis grows worse, gets better, or remains unchanged, is yet to be seen. Even if we see a recovery, we must face the reality that, ultimately, economic development on its current path is not sustainable. With increasingly rapid destruction of natural resources and the environment, where technology is used to create new demands rather than addressing real human needs and global debt continues to soar, it is just a matter of time before the next crisis looms. We may be somewhat assured that that the ruling elite, central bankers, corporate leaders, high ranking government leaders will have a plan. Perhaps as in the past, they will even orchestrate the crisis. As much as we like to believe our interests will be protected by our politicians, secret government agencies, and armed forces, don't count on it. What is more likely is that we serfs will continue to be just that...pawns who work to do the bidding of the powerful.

The trademark of a successful manufactured crisis is that the public will not only arrive at the expected course of action, they will insist upon it. One can predict with a high level of certainty that the puppet politicians and central banks will come to the rescue and enact a new economic and social order. We will probably get more of the same: wars, rebuilding, expansion, contraction, inflation, and deflation, all to keep us in constant struggle. Maybe the next major crisis will have a new twist with diseases or illnesses brought on by unhealthy things we consume requiring new cures will substitute for the destruction by war and subsequent rebuilding.

On the other hand, maybe the next disaster will be out of everyone's control. The question then becomes how people will respond. While economic collapse could lead to abject poverty, starvation, survival of the fittest, or totalitarianism, there is a chance that a New World Order will arise and bring about positive change; a new scientific based approach to sustainably utilizing the world's limited resources to meet the needs of all humanity and minimize its suffering. Rather than a science driven culture that contributes to our state of blasé, apathy, boredom and supports cruelty toward others, perhaps technology can provide the connection to support one another with the most effective use of the world's resources. Such altruism could bring us great freedom rather than the continued slavery from egoism.

So as socialistic as it may sound, people may need to elevate their thinking to a higher level beyond their own needs and security to one that addresses collective needs, regardless of what those who manipulate the paper and digits do. Ultimately, no matter what one's views are on religion, there is no simpler truth than loving thy neighbor as the best solution, but we may never know unless the whole system fails first. Perhaps there can be a silver lining to catastrophic economic collapse. People may get the opportunity to reinvent a system that sustainably addresses the needs of all as opposed to the few.

This would require breaking the long engrained social engineering, which prevents us to conceive of such a Golden Age, as they did in the time of the French Revolution. Perhaps it will take a true crisis to give us the courage to no longer be slaves to anxiety, repression, and bloodshed, or living passively by indulging in useless distraction.   The French used the term "ennui" to describe this condition where passivity and lack of imagination are tantamount to a form of damnation. Perhaps we can transform from this state to a Golden Age, but we must first break the shackles of deceit.

Epilogue

When I first started on my endeavor several years ago to explore what I believed to be a subtle but pervasive conspiracy in government and global financial systems, I was uncertain where it would lead. Over time, the scope of my project became so encompassing, to include not only government, but religion, history, economics, etc., that it became basically a philosophical exercise.

Despite evolution in my own thought process, there are certain premises to which I hold fast throughout. The first is that I am only wise to the extent that I realize how much I don't know. The second, is that it is still true what was proclaimed by former British Prime Minister Benjamin Disraeli a century ago that "the world is controlled by very different personages than believed by those who are not behind the scenes" and later asserted by former FBI Director J. Edgar Hoover that "the conspiracy in this country is so deep and so pervasive that even if the American people were to learn of it, they would not believe it". Undoubtedly, both were referring to the same secret societies decried by JFK decried in his speech just prior to his assassination. How are these secret societies connected with groups like the Illuminati, the Bilderbergs, the Trilaterals, the Skull and Bones, the Council on Foreign Relations, the Federal Reserve, the International Monetary Fund, and the multitude of secret and foreign government agencies? Does the money trail lead to the true architects of society? Are there arcane mystical or religious implications associated with these groups?

Do global events happen as a course of natural human progression? Are they part of a divine plan, or have self appointed kings asserted their secret dominion over most of civilization? Certainly ones views on God and Creation have the greatest influence on their view of the world. Faith allows man to achieve heroic acts of altruism, while others devoid of faith may acquire untold wealth and power by purist ego pursuits, completely unencumbered by the ethical standards imposed by religion. While some believe religious freedom is the most important and fundamental of human rights, others contend that it is a man made restraint that allows us to be manipulated and imposes the greatest limitation to our personal freedom.

Along the same lines, are Man and his science the measure of all things, or is there a higher authority by which our lives ought to be governed?   As Sigmund Freud suggests, our civilization is simply the culmination of conflict between the ego pursuits of self fulfilling happiness balanced against the altruistic struggle of the human species for survival.   Regardless of religious or philosophical beliefs, it is obvious that civilization can not exist without the off setting balance of love for others against egoism.   However, even as Freud suggests, we face a neurotic society under the pressure to maintain our civilization. We are locked in this enigmatic struggle between corporeal man and transcendent God.

With regard to what is real and what is fiction created to appear as reality, I hold to my beliefs that history as we know it is opinion, written from the perspective of the victor.   Wars are generally fought for economic reasons and the general population is controlled by fear and money.   Our money no longer real, just digits and paper backed by military might, which is why the U.S. and the Brits can run deficits in trillions. Ideological conflicts are real, but the populace functions only as pawns manipulated to follow the ideology of their leaders.   False flag operations have been used effectively to manipulate the masses to believe they are under attack. Perhaps as some believe, enemies provide a needed function for civilization, or maybe they simply help those remain in power with wars, destruction, peace and rebuilding in endless cycles.   But now that man has developed the means to annihilate the entire population of the planet, hopefully we will only engage in limited conflicts, so as to preserve civilization until the time of realization of the true meaning of our human existence or its natural demise.

Man's struggle for true freedom has been part of his nature since the beginning of written history.   But it is fear that now provides the greatest means of control over people and has been the greatest weapon used against us.   The media has continuously bombarded each and every home with messages of fear from all kinds of enemies who are dangerous to our well being, criminals, terrorists, diseases, etc. Our response has been to give up more freedom, all the while feeling an insidious loss of liberty.   Social engineering has fundamentally changed our relations with each other, even the basic relationships between men and women, as well as our religious well being.   If Life, Liberty and the

Pursuit of Happiness are inimical with serfdom, how do we free ourselves from those who control the money, arms and our teaching?

Along the same lines, is the fundamental question about truth and knowledge...What do we know as truth, and what are simply stories others have taught us as fact? One could take the position that we only know what we have experienced first hand and that all else becomes relegated as possibilities subject to distortion and limited by our faith. We will never know what we do not know, and we will never know what is beyond our own spatial-temporal capabilities. In the meantime, science marches forward in an effort to understand and control nature and our organic being, but along with each technological development comes a progression of dehumanization.

To all my readers, I wish you the best in your pursuit of the truth...continue to question and challenge! We may not be able to change the world, but we can always change our response to it. The more we can act in our collective interests, the less we allow other to dictate to us. We can also help wake others to the truth, so that the American dream does not become the American nightmare.

www.ingramcontent.com/pod-product-compliance
Lightning Source LLC
Chambersburg PA
CBHW061252280526
45784CB00002B/731